Existential Journalism

Humanistic Studies in the Communication Arts

Existential Journalism

by John Calhoun Merrill

COMMUNICATION ARTS BOOKS

HASTINGS HOUSE, PUBLISHERS
New York 10016

Library of Congress Cataloging in Publication Data

Merrill, John Calhoun, 1924-
   Existential journalism.

   (Humanistic studies in the communication arts)
(Communication arts books)
   Bibliography: p.   Includes index.
   1. Journalism—Philosophy. 2. Existentialism.
I. Title.
PN4731.M43 070.01 76-28806
ISBN 0-8038-1928-5
ISBN 0-8038-1929-3 pbk.

Published simultaneously in Canada by
Saunders of Toronto, LTd., Don Mills, Ontario

Printed in the United States of America

To
Daniel Schorr and Tom Wicker
representatives
of Kierkegaard's "Passionate Age"
that is fast disappearing

Importance of Inner Freedom

"The most important part of our freedom, inner freedom, is always subject to our will. If we surrender it to corruption, we do not deserve to be called human. But let us note that if the absolutely essential task is not political liberation, but the liberation of our souls from participation in the lie forced upon us, then it requires no physical, revolutionary, social, organizational measures, no meetings, strikes, trade unions—things fearful for us even to contemplate and from which we quite naturally allow circumstances to dissuade us. No! It requires from each individual a moral step within his power—*no more than that.* And no one who voluntarily runs with the hounds of falsehood, or props it up, will ever be able to justify himself to the living, or to posterity, or to his friends, or to his children."

— ALEXANDER I. SOLZHENITSYN
in *From Under the Rubble,* 1975.

Contents

4   **PESSIMISM, ANXIETY, AND FREEDOM**   68

5   **INDIVIDUALISM, COMMITMENT,
AND ACTION**   97

6   **IN SEARCH OF AUTHENTICITY**   118

7   **BACK TO NEWSROOM AND ACADEME**   139

Introduction

On the street where I live, journalism today is a "hot" item, and not in the way McLuhan uses the term.

Across the avenue, lines form nightly to watch heroes Hoffman and Redford unmake Richard M. Nixon in *All The President's Men*. Meanwhile, back at the ranch where I labor, the mails bring a surprising number of periodicals concerning the press—some with fancy names like the *Columbia Journalism Review* and some with more down-to-earth ones, like *More* and *Aim*. I have also lately received recent notice that citizen Spiro Agnew, of all people, is planning to publish a newsletter exposing the sins of the "media" and the barons who preside over them. Journalism departments and schools are not only among the most popular units of undergraduate universities, they are also accredited (and, one assumes, denied accreditation) by a gilt-edged association of elder statesmen concerned about the state of our newspapers and their role in our volatile culture. And the unpretentious journalism "sequence" over which I preside at a medium-sized suburban university turns up each year a good number of eager, intelligent, but almost invariably confused, youngsters who want to major in the arcana of journalism for reasons best known to themselves.

One would certainly never think, considering all these indices of a bull market in the pursuit of what Lady Gregory called "spreading the news," that American journalism is today probably approaching a critical stage of its evolution, one that will leave neither our daily newspapers nor nightly telecast in their present formats for long. In fact, these profound changes actually began more than twenty years ago and are simply gaining momentum at a time that is too late to do anything about them if we wanted to.

An *Introduction* to another writer's book is not the place to cite details and causes of modifications of cultural life, even if they are as important as the revolution in modern journalism going on around us at the moment. It is enough to note that most of the news mediated to Americans these days comes to them not from the print media but from broadcasting. We are, nevertheless, rushing inevitably towards the phenomenon of national newspapers (*The Wall Street Journal* is a bellwether), punctuated across the land by an increasing number of we-know-not-what sorts of dailies and weeklies covering local news and providing outlets for local advertisers. McLuhan notwithstanding, the print medium of news dissemination is almost certain to grow apace as our press localizes and specializes. Broadcasters will no doubt settle their journalistic functions upon what they do best: bringing us to far distant places and offering us the drama of instantaneous coverage of live events.

Headlines scream to us that doom is upon us and that, because of ecological imbalance, nuclear proliferation, pollution, poor health care, declining birth rates and other horrific facts of modernity *our* world, the world of the average citizen, is coming to an end, or at least that it is on the brink of falling into one or another ocean. How many journalists, however, know—or care to tell us—that *their* world is also in no less a precarious state than Western California? Most of them, like most of us cannot tell us what they have not yet realized. They live, for the most part, in the fictional land of yesterday, calling it "today," simply because it is an easy place to play games of pretense when important matters are at stake.

John Merrill is not this type of journalist—or citizen. In his earlier books and essays, Merrill's concerns have invariably centered upon the need for individuality in an age of organization men, for wholeness and commitment in a time of specialism and playing it safe. He stands for outright rebellion against those who would institutionalize or legalize our most precious possession, personal human responsibility for living meaningful lives.

What Merrill has been driving at all along, of course, is a concern that turns out to be philosophical in thrust, of special consequence to journalists in the unique ways that touch their particular (and colorful) type of work. That his focus is also, broadly speaking, "existential" is obvious, considering its accent upon individual choice, its distrust of determinism and somewhat gloomy nature and sly suspicions of the "safe creativity" that journalists (among others) attempt to inculcate in the young, both in their city rooms and on the nation's campuses. The appearance, therefore, of this volume, *Existential Journalism*, should come as no surprise to those familiar with Merrill's work. It merely is the inevitable outcome of his previous interests in the fog that surrounds such difficult notions as journalistic ethics and responsibilities of the press.

Like C.P. Snow, Merrill recognizes the peril of living at a time when journalism, like much culture, has been fractionalized by a tension between "self-reliance" (for lack of a better word) and "technique," as Ellul calls modern know-how. These analogues, centering upon the literary and scientific communities, eventually stimulate many questions when extended to journalistic endeavors, not the least of which is whether it is the duty of the nation's press to lead or follow the course of events; whether a free press in a capitalist society is competent to direct its own affairs without the constraints of rigid professionalization; whether reporters and editorialists are able to ingest the complexity of our culture, its odd specialisms and rapid changes with requisite expert sensitivity and intelligence. They also raise other critical concerns that, as recent history has demonstrated, *will* influence the course of our personal lives and probably those of our children.

Quite seriously and in perfectly good faith, determinists from Hegel to B.F. Skinner have answered, in one way or another, "no" to all of these questions. They ask us to make our errors, if we must make them, on the side of cold conservatism and not of idealism. Man is *not* a free agent in their view, nor has he ever been. He is merely a canny creature capable of deluding himself into poetic notions of liberty, possibly to scare away tyrannical demons of his true nature and narcotize the pathos of his mortal state, eventual non-being or death. For the time of our little ride here on the planet earth, they tell us, we had best attempt to legislate the *essences* of that which is best and most humane in our tradition, because these essences, in effect, determine the rules by which society must inevitably play its games for survival's sake.

While we have some flexibility in choosing *what* is indeed essential, our choice is limited by our own mortality. Becoming a monk, fleeing to the hills, composing a symphony or resorting to madness may delude us in our lonely prisons of self. But our days will nevertheless grind away, and both dictators and saints must finally pause and face identical trite puzzles about where we are going, deal with the same kinds of answers and not say too loudly, "Why?"

Kierkegaard was not the first thinker to rebel at this sort of doctinaire philosophy. He is one of the best known, because he asked his personal "Why?" at the right time: during a period of burgeoning economic, biological, and spiritual determinism. And later, in the years during and immediately after World War II, the flames of existential rebellion again burned high for similar but more dramatic reasons.

How well I remember the excitement I felt as a student at the Yale Drama School in late 1946 when Thornton Wilder turned up one day with a batch of plays from newly liberated France, plays by Sartre, Anouilh and others whose first names were invariably "Jean") and with the word, new to our ears, "existentialism" on his lips. With them arrived the writings of the first "new journalist," Camus. It seemed for the moment that somehow these thinkers, obsessed as they were with *living* each moment to the hilt in full awareness of the awful choices that freedom thrust upon them, were soon to liberate America from the creeping conformity and alienation from its own soul into which it was about to slide as a byproduct of the euphoria of victory.

The exchange seemed poetic: Just as France had found freedom under Nazi tyranny, so she would share her philosophical liberation with her democratic rescuers who now so sorely needed what she could offer them.

All of that was yesterday. Our hopes, predictions and dreams of that time were, I think, wrong. Existential embers smouldered, however. Now, a generation later, some—but not enough— American writers and intellectuals are asking themselves *de novo* almost the same questions that were once whispered from table to table in Left Bank bistros under the guns of the Germans.

History indeed sometimes repeats itself, and today different kinds of guns just beyond the horizon are taking aim at our culture. Silent revolutions begin these days when instruments that condition the minds of men, schools and mass media, are subverted by enemy forces who dress and act just like you and me, teach intentionally innocuous college classes, tell vapid jokes on video talk shows and compose the stylized front pages of our news-papers, all mechanistically performed with neither ideological commitment, zest for life nor a secular or spiritual vision of a meaningful, productive existence.

John Merrill will explain why these fears are not mere paranoia in the remaining pages of this book. *Existential Journalism* is a contribution to *Humanistic Studies in the Communication Arts* that I regard as both topical and vital, because its author has captured so pungently that same excitement and thirst for human freedom that I once knew so long ago in New Haven. The next step is for each of us to ingest Merrill's concerns and, like Anouilh's Antigone, act as we must at the harsh cost we will eventually pay anyway for the gift of life. *This* is the difficult part.

GEORGE N. GORDON, Ph.D.
Hofstra University

August, 1976

Preface

This volume is a follow-up or outgrowth of my *Imperative of Freedom* (1974) in which I tried, probably for the first time in American journalism literature, to point out the importance of the existentialist orientation in journalism. However, I went so far in weaving strands of rationalism and humanism (and even the Objectivism of Ayn Rand) into a philosophy of journalism, that for many readers, existentialism tended to get lost or at least submerged.

I did, however, lay most prominent stress on "freedom" and in so doing, played up one of the principal existential concerns. Many readers of the book did, interestingly, pick up the large concern with existentialism, and to some extent were critical of the book chiefly because of this emphasis. Especially was this true among my fellow journalism educators and among practicing journalists generally. They saw in the existential emphasis a danger: for in their minds lurked the suspicion—perhaps planted there during the turbulent 'sixties with the counterculture and youth revolution—that "radical" journalists who were trying to upset traditional values (and even the society itself) were those interested in existentialism. They remembered many of the youthful—and some not so youthful—rioters and dissidents, including many "underground" newspaper writers who had referred to themselves occasionally as "existentialists." So, to many readers of *The Imperative of Freedom*, I was encouraging anarchy in journalism—or worse, and filling the heads of students with erroneous and dangerous ideas. They were mainly reacting to their concepts of the term "existentialism," not having carefully read either my *Imperative of Freedom* nor known very much about existentialism as it had been seriously elucidated by its European founders and popularizers.

Nothing could have been further from the truth than that I was trying to enthrone "irresponsibility" in journalism. The very purpose of the book was to give an emphasis to *ethical* and responsible journalism as it had seldom been given before: from a philosophical perspective, one which, to be sure, emphasized the virtues of freedom, rationalism, and humanism. It is indeed strange that many readers (or were they really *readers*?) felt the philosophy espoused in the book was likely to lead to "irresponsibility" or relativistic ethics when probably the heaviest moral emphasis in the book was an explication of Kant's moral philosophy and its relationship to problems of journalism.

At any rate, the book served its purpose: to drive a philosophical wedge into the literature of American journalism and cause students and others to reexamine the fast-disappearing relevance of libertarianism both to the press system as a whole and to the individual journalist.

The present work continues this effort. However, here I shall limit the scope somewhat and focus on existentialism and its relevance to journalism. The attempt is made here to describe an "existential journalism" and to bring the term into the legitimate terminology of journalistic discussion. The intent in the pages which follow is to construct the basic framework of an existential journalism—and even, in so doing, to practice the spirit of the *genre* by passionately exhibiting by example (at least in spots) what I am talking about.

This exemplification of existential journalism while describing it, of course, leads to some problems, especially when such a volume as this falls into the traditional context of "academic" or "scholarly" prose. For example, there is no attempt made here to eschew the personal pronoun "I," and the reader will note it sprinkled throughout. This is certainly not conducive to "academic" prose. Also, in spots there is a language used which may well prove too "spirited" or "colorful" for many of my dispassionate and neutralist colleagues in Academe accustomed to prose which plods along to a "scientific" cadence.

Why a treatise on "Existential Journalism?" many readers

will ask. Will not this simply add another nebulous term to the literature of journalism? Is not such an emphasis already covered in books and articles on the so-called "New Journalism"?

These are reasonable questions, to be sure. My answer is briefly this: Other emphases in journalism in recent years have *not* really brought together the characteristics which coalesce in what I am calling "existential journalism." They have been either too general to be meaningful, or they have focused on some aspect of "New Journalism"—say, the writings of Tom Wolfe, or Gay Talese, or Norman Mailer—emphasizing *style* and *form*. Existential journalism, as I see it, is mainly a matter of *orientation* or *attitude*, which would, of course, manifest itself often in style and form but which is not mainly *literary* (as is one type of "New Journalism"). More will be said about this in Chapter 3. Existential journalism is basically a journalism which is practiced by existentialists who are journalists; it is a frame of mind—an attitude—which is thrust by individual journalists into their journalism, imbuing it with a vitality, a depth, a commitment, a character of flux, a creativity and originality which is almost universally lacking in modern "corporate" journalism.

Unfortunately, existentialism is largely misunderstood—or totally ignored—in the United States today. For many it conjures up thoughts of hedonism or anarchy, or is equated with a philosophy that justifies any and all immorality. It is, of course, not such a philosophy at all; rather it is a description of human freedom, and it explicitly requires and sets forth at every step a theory of responsibility and morality which shapes, and gives life to human freedom.

An example of a misrepresentation of existentialism can be found in an essay by Clare Boothe Luce[1] in which she equates existentialism with "doing your own thing," "anything goes"— including violence. She attributes the actions of Lynette ("Squeaky") Fromme—one of the "Manson Family"—to existentialism. Mrs. Luce proceeds to tie existentialism to liberalism and then to show that the whole bundle is "sick" and "irresponsible." I believe the views of Mrs. Luce are shared by many Americans who know little or nothing about existentialism. It is often made the scapegoat of every extreme, irresponsible action

---

[1] *The Wall Street Journal*, Sept. 24, 1975.

in today's world. Too often Sartre, especially (and other existentialists), are totally misrepresented. Sartre, admittedly one of the most "extreme" existentialists, has tried to establish through existentialism a philosophy of individual responsibility. Even though the world may seem absurd, man must create purpose for himself, using his abilities to the uttermost. To compare the "spaced-out" communal dependency of Haight-Asbury and the excesses of persons like "Squeaky" Fromme with the existentialism of the Continent is extremely far-fetched and unfair.

Mrs. Luce undoubtedly has many intellectual kindred spirits in schools and departments of journalism throughout the United States. It is unusual, indeed, to find a journalism teacher who sees much—if any—value to existentialism in journalism. He, like Mrs. Luce, most often equates such a stance with biased news, propaganda, subjectivity, editorializing, fictionalizing, irresponsibility—or something worse. He would purge journalists of the personal, of the ego, and would make them into "reporting machines" which set out to dispassionately "blot up" reality in what he refers to as "an objective manner." Although most journalism professors know little about existentialism, they are prejudiced against it and seek to so prejudice their students. Most journalism educators—and most journalists—in the United States today are *impersonalists* or *objectivists* giving short shrift to personal judgments and to subjective and committed (involved) journalism. They are basically *status quo* persons; they are at least psychological "collectivists" and organization men, suspicious or afraid of the Self and the stimulation and creativity that comes from "individual-oriented" journalism. This kind of journalism—that is, *existential* journalism—is seen by them as a danger because it "rocks the corporate boat" and endangers the smooth-running, *status quo*, impersonal journalism that is holding fast in this country.

It is against this "corporate" journalism, this depersonalized, conformist type of journalism that this volume strikes out. What we need is more emphasis on the individual journalist and on *his* freedom and *his* responsibility. (And when I say *his*, I mean *hers*, too.) We have enough emphasis on the freedom and responsibility of the journalistic *system*, and on the *mass media* themselves. We seem overly concerned about the system and the media retaining freedom from government or from other outside forces, but we are little concerned about the individual journalist who has become hardly more than a robot or conformist functionary of the journalistic enterprise for which he works. It is on this individual journalist that this work concentrates. For far too long he has been overlooked and neglected.

However, let me make it very clear that I am not optimistic about the individual journalist becoming an existentialist to the degree that it will cause profound changes in institutional journalism. Most journalists will sail placidly on in their comfortable, safe, lifeless, non-existential world, conforming and doing the same old things in virtually the same old ways. Only a few hearty souls will experience the truly existential level of journalism, and this number will be so few that the media managers and journalistic engineers need not worry about a breakdown in their "systems." Non-existential journalism will continue to be the rule in the United States (and in the entire world); conformity will continue to grow, and the armies of young people swarming out of journalism education programs eagerly seeking employment will gladly conform to the wishes of the managers and will adapt nicely to the highly regimented, depersonalized corporate structure of the mass media. They will, in essence, have died and been buried in the giant graveyards of modern Establishment Journalism. They will have their reward and their peace.

And they will join their older brothers and sisters of corporate journalism in pouring out for mass consumption large amounts of garbage: gossip, unsynthesized bits and snippets of this-and-that, sensation—much brainless, illiterate, superficial, meaningless—created chiefly for the entertainment-hungry, the lazy and the thoughtless. There is something wrong with today's journalism which is created by this mechanistic corps of non-existentialists; we all know it, but we have trouble articulating just what is wrong—or we refuse to admit openly how shallow and vapid American journalism really is. Arnold Rosenfeld, managing editor of _The Dayton_ (Ohio) _Daily News_ puts it this way:

> Readers look at newspapers, and what they feel in their gut is this: This has nothing to do with me. This newspaper is not in touch with life. It is in touch only with journalism and journalists. Nothing in it has been validated by anything I have seen or observed in my own life. I do not believe it. They express this

feeling in angry letters to the editor, in which they cannot articulate what they feel.[2]

The existential journalist rebels against being buried in this type of modern corporate journalism. He has an attitude of commitment, of rebellion, of individuality, of creativity, of freedom. He commits himself to himself and his own standards, not to the often asinine rules and practices of the organization. He pushes, straining constantly against the encompassing institutional restrictions which are closing in on him. He cares little about strict professionalism or institutionalism; more important to him is a sense of self-esteem and self-reliance. He takes stands; he chooses; and he is willing to take the consequences of these choices. This is often quite painful.

He suffers; he often stands alone; at times he is penalized—he is not promoted, he does not get the raise, he is put off over in some "corner" of the operation where he is "safe," and at times he loses his job. But he truly exists; he lives. He is no simple *thing* fitting snugly into the "system," functioning in cooperation with all the others for the production of some standard, unstimulating product. Or—if he does—he does it, fighting all the way. The existential journalist's lot is a difficult one in today's journalism, to be sure. Only occasionally will he be appreciated and rewarded by those in authority. But, of course, he *always* has his reward—the reward of existence, of truly living, itself. He wills, he chooses, he acts, he commits himself, he progresses: in effect, he *makes* himself daily. He is the existential journalist.

Journalistic "engagement" is the main thing. It has to do with involvement; it is the opposite from "standing apart from"; Sartre certainly stresses this: the existentialist is not a *disinterested* person; he is one who is involved, participating, feeling. But this surely does not mean that he is satisfied to thoughtlessly cooperate for the "sake of participating." For Sartre and other existentialists the key point is this: to be truly human is to be engaged; one must rebel at the idea of "standing at a distance." Existential journalism is not isolating oneself, trying to be some kind of recluse; rather it is plunging into dangerous waters and being willing to take chances.

Imitation is not engagement. It is a "cop out"; it is the way the

2 *The Bulletin* (ASNE), Nov./Dec., 1975, p. 8.

feeble and the unimaginative do their journalism. Certainly it is a comfortable and easy way; that is one reason it is so widely embraced. Listen to Eric Hoffer, not really an existentialist, writing about imitation:

> Imitation is often a shortcut to a solution. We copy when we lack the inclination, the ability or the time to work out an independent solution. People in a hurry will imitate more readily than people at leisure. Hustling thus tends to produce uniformity.[3]

Imitation is certainly related to conformity; those who imitate easily also tend to conform easily. Again, Eric Hoffer writes that "people whose lives are barren and insecure seem to show a greater willingness to obey than people who are self-sufficient and self-confident. To the frustrated, freedom from responsibility is more attractive than freedom from restraint."[4] This tendency to obey, to imitate, and to conform is very strong in society; and it is not strange that it is strong among journalists. Aldous Huxley believes there is a basic Will to Order among people, and this is actually dangerous, for it "can make tyrants out of those who merely aspire to clear up a mess," and also "the beauty of tidiness is used as a justification for despotism."[5] He goes on to say that "too much organization transforms men and women into automata, suffocates the creative spirit and abolishes the very possibility of freedom."[6]

The existential journalist rebels against this Will to Order and against what William Whyte (in *The Organization Man*) has called the "New Social Ethic." Whyte says the key words in this ethic are "adjustment," "adaptation," "social oriented behavior," "team work," "group loyalty," "group dynamics," "group think-ing," and "group creativity." I could add two others—especially pertinent to the field of journalism: *media loyalty* and *profes-sional spirit*.

Perhaps the journalist, as much as anyone in our society, is in a position to lose his selfhood and conform to what Lewis Yablonsky has called "robopathy."[7] He may feel himself crea-tive, but the nature of his work routinizes him into patterns of

---

[3] *The True Believer* (New York:Mentor Books, 1962), p. 96.
[4] *Ibid.*, p. 100.
[5] *Brave New World Revisited* (New York: Harper & Row—Perennial Library, 1965), p. 23.
[6] *Ibid.*
[7] *Robopaths: People as Machines* (Baltimore: Penguin Books, 1972.

activity devoid of creativity, challenge, spontaneity, and potency. His perception of the world is from the circumscribed view of the journalistic institution. He does his job, mechanically (or mechanistically) day after day without showing many—if any— sparks of creativity and passion. In fact, lack of passion—a *dispassionate* demeanor—is what defines his natural journalistic state.

He has either been educated to be dispassionate and routinized, or he has learned very quickly on the job in the newsroom. He learns "the way" things are done; he does them that way, and the work-flow moves smoothly along, and he is not pained nor troubled by unorthodox activities which create tensions and frictions. This he has learned well to evade. Life, he believes, is simpler, more "enjoyable," more placid, and less hectic if he conforms. In addition, he will not be pained by "making mistakes" and errors in judgment. And, what is more, he will more than likely be rewarded for being a good and cooperative staff member.

This person just described is the typical, the nonexistential, journalist. His number is legion. He conforms. He makes the usual marks; he interviews with the "normal" questions; he writes the regular "5-W" lead, and works his story into the standard "inverted pyramid" form. He submits his work to an editor who "corrects" it—modifying it in many ways, from subtle distortion to denuding it of its basic and original significance and meaning (if it had any). The nonexistential writer accepts this without protest—and continues to produce his rigid, superficial pieces with machinelike efficiency. He is, in effect, living an inauthentic life as a journalist; not only he, but the editor who "corrects" his copy, is locked into a system that denies their humanity and authenticity and enthrones routine and efficiency.

Very often, of course, journalists stir restlessly—at least some of them do, but in small ways with little avail, and then revert back into the security and harmony of conformity and passivity. The system dominates; corporate consciousness and power win out again and again over the individual. Creativity begins to mean nothing more than "conforming more efficiently," or doing the routine more skillfully and expeditiously. Of course, there are rebels in this system—the existentialists—who rebel persistently, but they make no real impact on the medium or the media system; they are "tolerated" for some reason, or they are

more directly ostracized from critical areas—or they are eliminated from the system altogether.

What normally happens to the journalist is described by
Yablonsky in his book on "robopaths":

> They find a successful mold, receive their rewards, and ritualisti-
> cally stick to it for the rest of their lives. They no longer put
> themselves "in harm's way" by branching out or trying a new and
> different approach. Their fears and lack of courage freeze them
> into static, uncreative roles, where they lock into a robopathic
> existence.[8]

Existential journalism may be thought of as a kind of
liberalism; certainly it is *future-oriented* like liberalism. And
with its emphasis on individualism, existentialism is liberalism
of a kind, but certainly a liberalism with no belief in a natural
social harmony and no hope for man's perfectibility. This is why
an existential journalist is leery of organizations, groups, press
councils, etc., along with professional ethical codes and sets of
"responsibilities" for the press, designed to define or codify
journalistic activities.

Not only does the existential journalist think that journalists
cannot be "perfected" by such groups and codes, but he actually
prizes the contentiousness, competitiveness and pluralism
which results from a lack of harmony both in his journalistic
enterprises and in society as a whole. So, it can be maintained
that the existential journalist, although very much a liberal in
some areas, also manifests many of the characteristics of the
twentieth-century "conservative."

Perhaps the most thorough and satisfying development of
existentialism in this century is contained in the writings of Karl
Jaspers. He sees the main danger to the individual in our highly
organized society as the growing desire to produce a standardized and conformist way of life for as many people as
possible. He has discussed this problem in many of his works,
but especially in his *Man in the Modern Age*, which I shall allude
to quite often later on. The main way a journalist can break out of
this conformist philosophy is to embrace the existentialist commitment to freedom, choosing, and living beyond himself. As
Sartre has said in a famous passage from *Being and Nothingness*,
"I am condemned to exist beyond my essence, beyond the

---

[8] *Ibid.*, p. 18.

causes and motives of my act. I am condemned to be free."[9] Lewis Mumford also emphasizes this necessity to constantly strike out anew in a continuous commitment; he writes in his *Transformations of Man* that "every goal man reaches provides a new starting point, and the sum of all man's days is just a beginning."[10]

Fewer and fewer journalists are living authentically in Sartre's freedom or cherishing Mumford's concept of constant future-plunging; journalists are settling for the comfort and rewards of conformity, of adjusting to the institutional system. It is not a happy future for the existentialist—or, perhaps a better way of expressing it, he is faced with ever-increasing challenges to authentic living. The direction of our society—and our journalism—does, indeed, look dismal. This is no reason, however, to lose hope. It should rather be a stimulus to commitment, to living as fully and passionately as possible.

The coming generation of journalists can fall further into the stultifying comfort which journalistic institutionalization has fashioned for them, and with a hopeless or resigned sigh consign their very personhoods to unruffled conformity and stability. Or, they can join the decimated ranks of existential journalists, reaffirm their selfhood, commit themselves to enlarging the frontiers of freedom and authenticity, and rise to higher and higher levels of existence.

---

[9] Raymond Van Over (ed.), *The Psychology of Freedom* (Greenwich, Conn.: Fawcett Premier Books, 1974), p. 320.

[10] *Transformations of Man* (New York: Harper Torchbooks, 1972), p. 192.

Voices from Newsroom
and Academe

THE THOUGHT CAME to me early in this project that perhaps I
was beating a dead horse—or better, a horse that did not
need beating at all. Could it be that the concept of "existential
journalism" was generally understood by journalists and journalism educators and was rather firmly entrenched in journalistic
parlance? I certainly did not think so, for I had seen the term
practically never, although perhaps many of the characteristics of
"existential journalism" (as I have come to understand it) do,
indeed, crop up here and there without the label. But I felt that
no significant core of meaning had developed around the term;
further, I felt that it *should have*, and a little prompting and pushing might be needed to set in motion a concern for existential
journalism—at least among a minority segment of the journalistic
community.

Naturally I was curious about meanings that journalists and
journalism educators had of "existential journalism." I set about
asking about the term—seeking meanings in a multitude of
informal contacts I had with teachers and practicing journalists.
But I also went beyond this face-to-face questioning. During
1975 I sent open-ended questionnaires to a small sample of
journalists and journalism professors in the United States. Fifty

forms were mailed out in late 1975 to educators in schools and departments of journalism and communications, and another 50 forms were sent to practicing journalists. Although the number of returned questionnaires was not particularly impressive, it was large enough to provide a good insight into the attitudes and meanings of the respondents. Twenty of the journalism educators responded, as compared to only 12 of the journalists. But their remarks were extremely interesting, and, I believe, reflect the various feelings about "existential journalism" held in the academic and journalistic communities.

Journalism professors seemed to try harder to answer the main question ("*What meaning do you give to the term 'existential journalism'? Please give main characteristics that come to mind or anything else you would like to say about the term.*") than did the journalists. Editors and other journalists responding were somewhat evasive and even noticably irritated at times by the questionnaire and at being asked for their meaning of the term.

The Journalists Speak

Let us look first, then, at some of the journalists' responses; these are rather typical of comments made by this group and indicate a mixture of mystification, irritation, and sarcasm, and—I might add—ignorance. I certainly realize however, that many of the responses may well be partially inspired by the fact that the journalists are busy (or *think* they are) and are very often annoyed by solicitations from the universities. Some few of the responses were downright hostile, and several of them, I think, evidence a widespread ignorance of what is going on in journalism education. I would really like to reply individually to some of the remarks made below by journalists, but shall pass up the temptation—at least at this point.

John Troutt, Jr., managing editor of the *Jonesboro* (Ark.) *Sun,* in giving the meaning which he attached to the term "existential journalism," wrote:

> Although I will probably be branded a hopeless rube, I must reply that I don't have the faintest idea what the term "existential journalism" might mean. I would also doubt that it is very important in the overall scheme of things.

Robert J. Bailyn, editor of *The News-Times*, Danbury, Conn., responded in these words:

> No doubt we're rather backwards in the Berkshire foothills. But a quick survey of the newsroom uncovered no one who had the Sartre-ist notion what "existential" journalism is. Is it that we here are locked in the private hell of our newsroom, condemned to face each other and ourselves for eternity, with no access to Olympic journalistic thought?

Jack Spalding, of the *Atlanta Journal*, defined the term in one word: "transitory." And Ladd Hamilton, managing editor of the *Lewiston* (Idaho) *Morning Tribune*, evidencing a growing criticism of journalism students and an impatience with answering questionnaires, wrote:

> We are getting people out of the journalism schools who can't spell, who can't compose a lead and never heard of libel, and you ask me to share your concern about existential journalism. I've never heard of it, I haven't got the time to look it up, and I doubt whether it has anything to do with the real world of writing and editing—or the teaching thereof.

Mike Lavelle of *The Chicago Tribune*, also, showed his annoyance with the questionnaire and with the whole subject. And he replied with pungent sarcasm and strained humor:

> Existentialism and a ham sandwich—will get you a ham sandwich. I don't think it's sensible to define journalism in intellectual terms that more correctly belong within the field of the novelist as they relate to a philosophical train of thought—i.e., Dostoevsky, Camus, Sartre, Ibsen, Melville. Journalism has, or ought to have an immediate impact on social problems in the sense that the Hegelian engine will not slow down to deal with such mundane issues that I and Kenan Heise (of the Trib's Action Line) have to deal with. One doesn't tell a welfare mother or an unemployed worker that they are "Part of History," that is the function of the novelist who generally writes of things that were rather than of things that are. If you catch me when I am (if I make it) in my sixties I might be able to define what I thought I was doing in heavy metaphysical terms, but for the present I am too busy doing whatever I do, to bother with what I think I think I'm doing.

Kendall Wild of the *Rutland* (Vt.) *Daily Hearld* wrote that he had never heard of "existential journalism." But he proceeded to list some things he had heard of, and these perhaps, give some inkling of his concept of the term. He had, by the way, heard of advocacy journalism, macho journalism, yellow journalism, dumb journalism, cop-out journalism, new journalism, provincial journalism, big-city journalism, slick journalism, and good journalism. He then proceeded to ask what "existential journalism" is; is it, he poses, "when you send stories to the composing room and wonder what they'll look like when they appear in the paper?" Or—"is it feature stories on Jean-Paul Sartre?"

The editor of *The Charlotte* (N.C.) *Observer*, C. A. McKnight, wrote: "I tried your 'existential journalism' on more than 20 editors and writers in my news room and one journalism faculty member at Chapel Hill. No one had ever heard the phrase before."

From Miami, Jim Dance of *The Miami Herald* wrote that he and his staff were unable to give a meaningful defintion of "existential journalism." He responded:

It would appear that despite our newspaper experience, we are non-existential in the field of journalism—and this despite the presence on our staff of a callow 37-year-old editorial writer who came to us, direct, during the last year from a school of journalism where he taught.

Joe H. Stroud, editor of the *Detroit Free Press*, reinforces the puzzlement most of the journalists found with the term. He wrote:

Existential journalism is a phrase that has absolutely no meaning for me. I understand the generalized meanings of existential philosophy, but have not heard it applied to a particular form of journalism. I asked several of my colleagues, including one who is especially well read in existentialism, and they profess similar frustration over the phrase.

Probably the most serious attempt to respond to the question naire was made by Keith Coulbourn, a staff writer for the *Atlanta Journal-Constitution Magazine*. In part this is his reply:

Seriously, I never heard the term "existential journalism" before and hope that I never hear it again. Something *does* come to mind, of course, but since I've gone rather heavily into Wittenstein and that bunch my impressions are almost all negative. I associate the term with that mind-rotting moodism produced mainly on the Continent and at Northwestern University. Actually there's a rough overlap in one small aspect of it with our good ole American Pragmatism; it's called "phenomenology." But even here the existentialist goes off the deep end, striving as he does to reach "raw experience" or the "basic structure of experience" untouched by culture, etc.

I don't believe you can have an "existential journalism" as such, but only a journalism with a relatively high degree of existential elements. There's always been some degree of that in good writing, including journalism, because it features a certain attitude of organic oneness, a sympathy or empathy that fuses subject and object (transcending the Indo-European subject-object split, one might say) and seeming to place man (or at least the writer) at the exact center of the universe. It's an intellectual emotionalism, terribly subjective and hard to do well. Even a pro like Mailer often becomes bombastic, mawkish and silly. The worst part about it is that if you take most of that long, rambling stuff and turn it into simple sentences, almost all of it evaporates at room temperature.

And, as the final representative of the journalists, Earl W. Foell, managing editor of *The Christian Science Monitor*, offered these wrods:

Alas, alas, I'm sorry to say the phrase "existential journalism" has not penetrated to this isolated Eastern outpost. We are still stuck with discussing such outmoded issues as "participatory journalism" and whether Tom Wolfe should go back to reenliven his old night beat on the *Springfield Union*. Even at the recent AP Managing Editors' conference in Williamsburg, where editors from across the country met for their annual discussion of journalistic issues, not a word was heard about "existential journalism." So, with apologies to Sartre and you, this questionnaire will have to go unanswered.

The Journalism Educators Speak

Now, with the humor, sarcasm, and general ignorance of the journalists laid bare, let us turn to my fellow journalism educators. Many of them evidence the same impatience with the subject; and most of them were equally bewildered as to the meaning of the term. But, generally, they made a more conscientious attempt to give the term a meaning—which may, of course, simply evidence the widespread proclivity of academic types to appear informed whether they are or not.

At any rate, here are examples of the replies received:

John DeMott, of Temple University, did not like the sound of the term "existential journalism" which he related to journalism which is not "objective." He wrote:

Existential journalism is a contradiction in terms, really. Why? Because the essence of journalism is its objectivity. Now we all know, and concede readily, that no journalist can be 100 per cent objective. Or 100 per cent fair. Or truthful. Or accurate. Or anything else. However, an account of any "news" development is journalistic—rather than existential—it appears to me, to the degree that it corresponds to the relevant objective reality. If it's primarily an expression of the "reporter's" subjective reaction to the news event, or an opinion concerning it, then it's not journalism, in a professional sense.

The personal "journal," which I see as the principal instrument of "existential journalism" is a legitimate part of any news medium's overall content. However, the personal journal or personal journalism is more or less the antithesis of professional journalism and its fundamental function, because the faithful and competent performance of that function requires a religious-like commitment to non-commitment, a deep involvement in non-involvement, a strong partiality towards non-partisanship, and an aggressive pursuit of neutrality. All those concepts—paradoxes, yes, in many ways—appear nonsensical or hypocritical to the "existential" journalist, who glories in an austistic scorn of objective reality, rather than a strenuous effort to get outside or rise above his own convictions or biases.

L. John Martin, University of Maryland, provided this comment:

I have never heard the term "existential journalism" and neither has anyone else on my faculty. If it is in any way related to existentialism, I would guess that you are referring to the trend in subjective, descriptive journalism often referred to as new non-fiction. It would cover any journalistic writing that is not primarily concerned with truth as an absolute but with truth as it is seen by the reporter. Objectivity would be irrelevent in this type of journalism since it would contradict the underlying philosophy associated with "existential journalism." Objectivity is impersonal, while "existential journalism" by this definition is very personal.

Daniel Garvey, University of California, Long Beach, responded to the question in these words:

I haven't the slightest idea what existential journalism is. I have never been sure what existentialism is (or, perhaps, was), and I doubt that I can really say what journalism is (or, perhaps, was.) I would think that "existential journalism" would be a highly subjective kind of journalism, one in which the journalist relies entirely upon his own impressions for "facts." Reality and truth would be entirely the "reality and truth" and facts from other sources would be accepted only to the extent that the journalist could accommodate those opinions and facts within his own sphere of "reality." I assume too that existential journalism would perceive existence as essentially pointless. Thus, the import we attach to certain stories would probably be lost. Stories of human suffering and catastrophe would probably be given less play, greeted with more of a "so what" attitude. Angry and strident journalism would have no place. Harking to Kierkegaard, little import would be given to history. Yesterday's truth may not be today's truth, and only today's truth has meaning. Overall, I'm not sure it would be such a bad kind of journalism.

Don Ranly, University of Missouri, after a paragraph of generalized comment about "existentialism," concluded with this brief meaning which he attached to "existential journalism":

> Applying this to "existential journalism" is not difficult. The existential journalist does not give in to pressures, does not conform, is committed to being himself, to being free, and ultimately and always to truth.

One other Missouri professor's concept of existential journalism should be mentioned. Ralph Lowenstein* believed that an existential journalist "is one who writes totally from his own point of view, giving full vent to his own biases on the subject approached." Lowenstein continued describing the existential journalist:

> He is interested in expressing *himself*, exercising literary license and beyond to give the feel of the event, as well as what he perceives to be the facts of the event. He is not concerned with presenting all the facts, or even the variety of facts that the average reporter could gather. Primarily, his intent is to assimilate the facts of an event and his own inner consciousness to present a story in such a way that the reader will see this clearly defined, deep point of view in the same way that the writer sees it.

> Such writing is like a laser beam, focusing all its strength on one point, increasing its power a thousand-fold. The existential writer would not be bothered if some other existential writer produced the other point of view (or another point of view) in the same way. He would probably be delighted, because he would not delude himself into believing that any one person could present the whole truth.

---

* As of September 1976 Dr. Lowenstein is Dean of the College of Journalism and Communications, University of Florida.

Karlen Mooradian, of the University of Oklahoma, presented his concept of "existential journalism" in these words:

Existentialism has numerous meanings, but the ones I associate with it include: a protest against concepts that de-personalize the human individual and render him unable to "be himself" due to the centralized might of technology, "mass culture," and political systems; the emphasis on free will as opposed to merely reason; and the idea that since knowledge cannot transcend experience, the individual possesses but a short time-span and thus cannot formulate an overall philosophical strategy. I feel that existential journalism, without necessarily being conscious of itself as such, may become more prevalent if society continues to produce anxieties, dehumanization and cynicism (as opposed to skepticism) on as broad scale as currently.

Al Hester, University of Georgia, wrote that he was "uncomfortable with 'labels' and that 'existential' is a very fuzzy word." He goes on to say:

If "existential journalism" is taken to mean the type of journalism in which the journalist feels he/she can influence events and institutions by what he/she writes, then I can see some utility in the term. I would also, I think, probably consider that existential journalism would be the journalism of personal involvement, of intuitive writing about events, etc. We obviously see journalists who owe their allegiance to truths obtained through intuition, the emotions, "gut-feelings," etc.

Mort Stern, University of Colorado, replied that he does not use the term; "I associate it with nothing," he wrote. Everette Dennis, University of Minnesota, believed existential journalism is "a kind of mix of heart and head among intellectuals in journalism who tend to express themselves in thoughtful polemics." And, Wilbur Doctor, of the University of Rhode Island, wrote that he had never heard the term previously, and then decried the fact that he would now "have to worry about this deficiency" in his education means.

David M. Rubin, of New York University, replied that he was "stumped" by the term, but that he would be interested to hear just what existential journalism is.

Hanno Hardt, of the University of Iowa, seemed to be the one journalism professor polled who thought he had a grasp of the term's meaning. He even went so far as to enclose a paper he had written ("The Dilemma of Mass Communication: An Existentialist View") which went into the relationship of existentialism to mass communication, drawing very heavily on the concepts of Martin Heidegger. Some of Hardt's ideas will be referred to later in this volume.

Concluding the examples of journalism professors and their meanings for "existential journalism," here are the thoughtful and succinct remarks of Patricia A. Larsen, of Central Missouri State University:

> I interpret "existential journalism" as journalism with a reporter's direct involvement—an intellectual approach, not objective as we admonish our beginning news reporters to be, but subjective. It's every man (or woman) for himself/herself type of thing; and yet, each is responsible for his/her actions.
>
> Existential journalism is freedom personified; however, where the journalist has no freedom, he has no ethics. I believe existential journalism is becoming more prevalent. . . . I see the trend as good. But it is good only if the journalist gives all sides of the issue, problem and story. So his, or her, involvement must be on many levels and with many people.

*   *   *

In the second question of the questionnaire, respondents were asked to name journalists (and journals) in the United States or abroad—contemporary or in the past—which they associated with existential journalism. The practicing journalists did not name a single one; again, the journalism educators were far more responsive.

Persons who were named as exemplary of existential journalism were these: Norman Mailer, Truman Capote, Tom Wolfe, Hunter Thompson, Herbert Schiller, I. F. Stone, Gay Talese, Jimmy Breslin, Abbie Hoffman, Terry Southern, George Plimpton, Søren Kierkegaard, Karl Jaspers, Edmund Husserl, Martin Heidegger, and Jean-Paul Sartre. Journals listed were *East Village Other, The Village Voice, Rolling Stone, Los Angeles Free Press, Berkeley Barb, New York Magazine, I.F. Stone's Weekly, Commentary,* and *Commonweal.*

It is interesting that most respondents associated existential journalism with the "underground press" or with some form of "New Journalism." It is also interesting that no respondent named as "existential journalists" such people as Albert Camus, Henry David Thoreau, H. L. Mencken, Walt Whitman, Ernest Hemingway, Edward R. Murrow, Drew Pearson, Tom Wicker, and Daniel Schorr. These are certainly examples which I would give, and which I feel typify the spirit of existentialism in journalism which I shall try to explicate in the following pages.

Three things were shown rather clearly from the questionnaires returned: (1) the term "existential journalism" is completely meaningless to many in journalism, (2) the term is nebulously connected with "New Journalism" in the minds of many, and (3) the term is extremely fuzzy and/or unimportant in the minds of many others.

Some Concluding Remarks

The responses came as no real surprise. Ignorance of, or confusion about, the term "existential journalism" was expected. This is the very reason I wanted to write about the subject: to try to clarify—or isolate—the term and give it some meaning. And, what is more, I hoped by so doing, to give the concept some *importance*. I do think existential journalism can be given a rather distinct meaning, and certainly I think it is an important concept to journalists, journalism professors, and journalism students. Unlike some of the respondents—especially those actively engaged (and I use those words loosely) in journalism—I think intellectual concerns in journalism are more important in the long run than the repetitious, routine, imitative, unthinking kind of journalistic busy-work practiced all too generally in the United States.

I hope that on the following pages I can present a meaningful outline of existential journalism, and at the same time convey the importance I attach to the orientation. Certainly there is some overlap between existential journalism and New Journalism in some of its types; but existential journalism is something more— and something *more important* and *lasting*—than New Journalism. Existential journalism was here before New Journalism and will be here after "the fad of the 60's" is long gone. Existential journalism is something, for example, which permeates segments of *all kinds* of journalism, not just counterculture journals, or literary journals, or political journals, or "liberal" journals. It can be found anywhere journalism is practiced. It is often hard to find, but chances are it is there, exemplified by persons without the big reputations of the Mailers, Wolfes, and the Stones. It has to do with intellectual and psychological "life-styles" of freedom and self-respect—

not with "literary" proficiency, anti-government stances, use of four-letter words and the like.

It is sincerely hoped that this volume will help bring the *issue* of existential journalism into focus. There is no real desire—or hope—that many journalists will become "existential" because of this volume or, for that matter, that many will even agree with the existential emphasis presented here. It is my belief—and it undobutedly stems from my basic existential foundation of pessimism—that most journalists are perfectly satisfied with the kind of journalism they are producing, just as most Americans are satisfied with the kind of journalism they are getting. Most journalists, I believe, like their "corporate" image, their comfortable niches in their complacent professionalism. Notice that I say "most" journalists like their "non-existential" situation; there are *some*, of course, who do not. And it is with this minority of existential journalists that I find stimulation and personal satisfaction—but, I must repeat, I do not find any real *hope* for the transformation of journalism by this tiny group of authentic journalists. The grip on journalism of the "ABC's"—Anonymity, Bigness, and Conformity—is simply too powerful to break loose from.

If the above sounds callous or pessimistic—or both—it is not really intended to be so; such words simply stem from my recognition of realities of workaday journalism and the proclivities of the modern spirit of collectivism and cooperation. It also stems from my seeing all around me the de-emphasis of the humanities and the constant glorification of, and reliance on, the sciences—a trend which has invaded journalism—and especially journalism *education*—with a vengeance. In spite of this de-emphasis of the artistic spirit in favor of a more scientific one, there is still in journalism, and in journalism education, the two basic orientations or stances. Let us take a look at them now.

Basic Journalistic Stances

I am a great believer in the device, practiced by most responsible American newspapers, of separating the news developments and the newspaper's editorial opinion. The first should be a flat, unembroidered account of the facts surrounding the items of news. It should be, so far as is humanly possible, free from the writer's or the commentator's personal interpretation or views.

—BARRY GOLDWATER, *The Conscience of a Majority*

Objectivity is not, as it is often implied in a false idea of "scientific" objectivity, synonymous with detachment, with absence of interest and care. How can one penetrate the veiling surface of things to their causes and relationship if one does not have an interest that is vital and sufficiently impelling for so laborious a task?

—ERICH FROMM, *Man for Himself*

THE TRAITS OR characteristics of journalists which help define their existential or non-existential natures are, of course, many and complex. They overlap in many cases and are otherwise difficult to isolate and discuss; but before getting into the main body of this work which discusses *existential journalism* in some detail, it might be well to deal briefly with journalistic stances or orientations which are most common today. Affecting the work of journalists today is a wide assortment of interests, ideologies, educational levels and cultural backgrounds, special talents, and so on. This is true even in societies where conformity and institutionalism have led to highly monolithic press systems.

It is certainly true in American society. The journalist in any society—but especially in a libertarian or quasi-libertarian society—is a many-sided person with several strong traits and tendencies. But even though all this is true, there seems to be in all journalists a basic and dominant psycho-ideological orientation which is either tilting in the direction of existentialism or away from existentialism. And it tends to manifest itself in most of the journalist's thinking and action.

Before getting more specifically into existential journalism *per se* in the following chapters, let us consider some of these basic stances which are found among journalists. One's orientation, undoubtedly, has a great deal to do with the kind of outlook one adopts as a journalist and even with stylistic characteristics of his journalism. In fact, his orientation affects his total journalistic *Weltanschauung*, for it leads him to consider certain fundamental issues related to journalism in ways consistent with this orientation. His basic stance indicates to a large degree his proclivity toward existentialism or against it. That is why it might be well to look at these stances here.

A journalist normally writes the way he thinks; he generally thinks according to his psycho-ideological orientation. A journalist, of course, may have mixture of orientations, but one will usually dominate. The problem comes when we attempt to classify orientations, but it can be done. And, although there are innumerable ways to set up such classification systems, the tendency is for all such systems to gravitate into two journalistic orientational types: (1) the mainly *objective* (scientific) journalist and (2) the mainly *subjective* (artistic) journalist. The second of these is to a large extent what I am referring to here as the *existential* journalist. This dichotomy will likely not satisfy everybody, but over the years while doing and teaching journalism, I have come to believe that these are the two main orientations or stances. It is not a matter always of "either-or"; rather it is a matter of dominant orientation, of a particular journalist being predominantly scientifically oriented or being predominantly artistically oriented. These two main tendencies will be taken up later in this chapter.

First, let us consider briefly several of the dualistic classifications into which basic orientations or stances may fall. Others are suggested in the figure ("Basic Journalistic Orientations") to be found later in the chapter.

Several Dichotomous Stances

One immediate problem with discussing stances is that there are so many dualistic classifications which can be used. There is, then, the problem of selection. And there is the more philosophical problem, emphasized in General Semantics, of the logical weakness of binary classifications: with such classifications we are certain to do injustice to reality, for the "either-or" typology leads to distorted and simplistic thinking about the nature of the subject being classified. Naturally these are both formidable problems and each, in its own way, tends to distort reality. However, it must be noted that *any* system of classification (or of language usage in any form) distorts reality and is unsatisfactory in some sense. But in spite of the weaknesses of typologies, and the warnings of General Semanticists notwithstanding, I shall discuss journalistic orientations by "types"—with considerable emphasis given to dualistic generalizations.

For me, a larger problem than the *semantic* weakness inherent in a binary classification is the problem of *selection* of these dualistic classifications. Journalists may be oriented primarily in dozens of ways which have approximate "opposites." What, then, are the most significant of these ways? This is the question which has haunted me, and it is quite possible that better classifications (more useful for analysis) could be used, but these which follow should at least serve as catalysts for disagreement even if they do not provide for everyone a personally satisfying method for understanding journalistic stances. And, it is my belief that in dealing with these several dualistic stances, there are some that are mainly *non-existential* and others that go together to coalesce into a rather clear *existential* orientation.

THE "INVOLVED" AND ALOOF STANCES

This is a very basic and common way of considering journalists in binary fashion. The 'involved" journalist is generally considered one who is oriented to participating, to activism, to being personally and emotionally involved in the events of the day. He does not believe in neutrality for the journalist; he thinks it desirable that he bring his own ideological beliefs, preferences and biases to bear on his journalism. He is the person many refer to as the "activist" journalist who, as J. K. Hvistendahl says, "looks at traditional reporting as being sterile and . . . considers reporters who refuse to commit themselves to a point of view as being cynical or hypocritical."[1] Hvistendahl goes on to say that "truth-as-I-see it" reporting might be a more accurate description of this new trend in journalism than "activist reporting" for these "new" journalists believe that the reporter who is seeking the truth should report the truth *as they see it*. The *involved* journalist, as I prefer to call him here, desires to bring himself, his intelligence, his sensitivites, his judgments to bear on the news of the day; he is not satisfied to be a mere bystander, an objective observer, a recorder or a neutralist.

The journalist with the *aloof orientation*, on the other hand, maintains that journalism is primarily a disinterested activity where audiences should not be encumbered by the journalists' biases, prejudices, judgments, feelings and opinions. The journalist with the *aloof* orientation is often called the "objective" journalist (see Chapter 1), although this is probably a misnomer. But he does subscribe to the Neutralist Position whereby the journalist keeps himself and his opinions and judgments out of his journalism—or tries to. This is still a dominant orientation in the United States and is fostered in schools and departments of journalism—although it did have a shot of new vigor injected into it by subjectivists and activists during the 1960's. Much of this personalism still clings to large segments of the American press.[2]

THE "DIONYSIAN" AND "APOLLONIAN" STANCES

Another interesting and useful dualistic way to describe one's journalistic stance is to categorize him as either "Dionysian" or "Apollonian." These are the dichotomous tendencies toward emotion on one hand and toward reason on the other. This dualism was first highlighted in these terms by Nietzsche in *The Birth of Tragedy from the Spirit of Music*. He observed two opposite elements in Greek tragedies and believed them to be

---

[1] "The Reporter as Activist: Fourth Revolution in Journalism," *The Quill* (Feb. 1970), p. 8.

[2] The influence of such writers as Gay Talese, Gail Sheehy, Larry King, Willie Morris, Norman Mailer, Tom Wolfe, Truman Capote and Robert Daley were especially influential in the "New" journalism during the 1960's and into the 1970's.

basic metaphysical principles in reality. Nietzsche named them for two Greek gods—Apollo, the god of light, and Dionysus, the god of wine.

Dionysus can be thought of as a symbol for emotion, mysticism, a free and unfettered spirit, intuition, irrationality, and a kind of darkness. Apollo, on the other hand, is symbolic of reason, beauty, order, wisdom, and light.

Nietzsche, it seems, considered Apollo (Reason) a necessary element, but unreliable and thus an inferior guide to existence; in other words, he believed that such an orientation provides man an inadequate view of reality. In many ways, therefore, Nietzsche might be called the "Father of Existential Journalism." For Nietzsche the symbol of Dionysus is superior to that of Apollo, for Dionysus is the free spirit that offers man, through some kind of mysterious sensitivity or intuition, a more valid and profound vision of reality.

The "Poetic" and "Prosaic" Stances

A third dualistic classification of journalists might be constructed on the basis of their stylistic proclivities. Some journalists, of the Dionysian type discussed above, tend to subjectivize their journalism in an attempt to get beneath the surface of reality and present a fuller and more authentic picture. These are the *poetic* journalists. Other journalists, largely Apollonian, are content with the more traditional style of expression common among journalists who have adopted what might be termed "the wire-service" style.

This basic difference in communicative expression stems from the dominant orientation accepted by the journalists: poetic (a kind of "open" or flexible style) or prosaic (a kind of "closed" or mechanistic style). The Poetic Journalist is more personal or individual and less dogmatic in his style than is his counterpart. Also, he is more "impressionistic." He is willing to experiment with his journalism, especially in matters of story form and style. He is not as "hemmed in" by normal or traditional practices as is the more disciplined Prosaic Journalist. He is not very concerned about keeping himself out of his story; in fact he delights in giving his journalism the stamp of his own individual personality. He places great importance on his own ability to adapt his style to the story, and has great respect for self-expression, freedom, and autonomy.[3]

The *Prosaic Journalist*, on the other hand, is a believer in facts. He stresses literalness and explicit statements; he is interested in the accuracy of his stories—at least in the accuracy of what he selects to be in his stories. He praises what he calls "objectivity," considering it the same as reliability and truthfulness. The prosaic mind, according to George W. Morgan, considers the objective as identical with the factual. "In addition, and most important," Morgan writes, "it is believed that to be objective means to withhold the feelings and to be detached and impersonal."[4]

As Morgan rightly points out, facts are important to a person (and certainly to a journalist), but they can be overstressed to the detriment of other things which are equally important. For example, Morgan says that persons with "prosaic minds" tend to have little respect for interpretation "because it appears incompatible with fact: fact is what *is*, they think, while interpretation is whatever one makes it; facts are believed to be objective, and interpretation, subjective." Morgan notes that for prosaic persons, knowledge of facts—no matter how isolated, irrelevant or minuscule—becomes genuine knowledge and interpretation becomes prejudice; for the journalist with this orientation, "sticking to the facts" is the height of responsibility—anything else is "irresponsible fancy."[5]

THE "PERSONALIST" AND "FACTUALIST" STANCES

These orientations are quite similar to the poetic and prosaic discussed above except that they relate to the total outlook on journalism and its purpose, going beyond the simple *style* of the journalism. The Personalist is the "people-oriented" journalist who makes most decisions on the basis of the way he thinks they will affect *people*—including himself. His main concern is with

---

[3] For a discussion of "psychic openness" and other characteristics of the communication style of the Poetic Journalist, see Chapter 6 ("Style: The Dimension of Self") in A. Donald Bell and J. C. Merrill, *Dimensions of Christian Writing* (Grand Rapids, Mich.: Zondervan Publishing House, 1970).

[4] George W. Morgan, *The Human Predicament* (New York: Dell Publishing Co.—a Delta Book, 1970), p. 83.

[5] *Ibid.*, p. 88.

people, and he takes their feelings and sensitivities into consideration before he writes a story or gives it a certain emphasis in the news. People are always at the center of his journalism, and in an important way he is a utilitarian for he is thinking of consequences. In other words, the Personalist will be largely controlled by his sensitivity to people connected with the story; this is very much an "involved" or "subjective" stance and is at variance with what might be called *factualism*—or the orientation of dispassionate neutralism which focuses on *what* was said or done.[6]

The Factualist is one who is oriented toward journalistic aloofness or neutralism, taking a kind of prosaic position in his communication style. He concentrates on the facts, the events themselves, on what happened, on what people say, and the like. The *what* of the story is more important than the *why*—even if the *what* is simply an accurate accounting of somebody else's version of what happened, or somebody else's opinion. Although the Factualist is usually considered the "objective" journalist, having varying degrees of suspicion of, or hostility to, what he sees as involved, evaluative or subjective journalism. He tries diligently not to become involved in his story—or with the people of his story. His is the orientation of detachment, at least from personal opinions, attitudes or biases for self or for others so that his subjective feelings will not determine what he considers news or how he presents it. Facts to the Factualist are sacred; they are to be presented dispassionately and accurately, and if they are, the audience member should get the best possible picture of the total event, unadorned by the ideological and psychological biases of the reporter and editor.

THE "EXISTENTIAL" AND "RATIONAL" SUPER-STANCES

In a way, all the preceding orientations coalesce into either existential or rational emphases. The basic questions behind these stances seem to be: How involved and committed should journalists be? What is reality and how should journalists best get at it? And, finally, how should they pass on such "reality-

---

[6] For a more extended discussion of people-oriented and fact-oriented journalists, see J. C. Merrill and R. L. Lowenstein, *Media, Messages, and Men* (New York: David McKay, 1971), pp. 244-46.

information"? Earlier, the existential orientation was related to the Dionysian, and the rational orientation to the Apollonian. Just as easily, we might refer to the existential orientation as Romantic and the rational orientation as Platonic. It is basically the old conflict between Emotion (Intuition) and Reason (Logic). Also, we might connect the Artistic orientation with existential orientation, and the Prosaic (or Scientific) with the Rationalist.

At the risk of confusing the issue, we could further postulate that an *intellectual* orientation is closely related to existentialism. The term "intellectual," however, is enshrouded in more semantic fog than almost any term we could use, and it is difficult to speak of a journalist with an "intellectual" orientation. C. Wright Mills sees the intellectual journalist as somewhat akin to the existentialist because he has a tragic sense of life.[7] He realizes that grassroots democratic controls have become practically nonexistent—at least minimized—and that seemingly irresponsible actions by persons at the top are permitted—even encouraged—by The System. Others are dependent on the Leaders and must suffer the consequences of their ignorance and mistakes, their self-deceptions and their biased motives. It is the recognition of this that gives the Intellectual a sense of tragedy.

The intellectual journalist easily becomes frustrated, for too often he has gained the illusion that his thinking and concerns make a real difference in the affairs of society; he slowly wakes up to the fact that this is not really the case. But even though the Intellectual may have some characteristics in common with the existentialist, he is often quite different. For instance, the existentialist would fight harder than the Intellectual for freedom and autonomy; he would not "give up" as quickly. According to Mills, the intellectual person is a slave to somebody or some policy, and, although he may exercise a limited amount of freedom in his actions, he knows he must not go beyond these limits. He must ever watch his step. He must pull his punches to keep from offending his editor, his publisher, or some powerful person or group in his community. In many cases the intellectual journalist has adapted to these pressures, to these restricting forces, and has tried to confine his "creativity" and "individual-

---

[7] See C. Wright Mills, "The Social Role of the Intellectual," Ch. 3 in *Power, Politics and People* (New York: Ballentine Books, 1962). For another excellent discussion of this subject in relation to journalism, see Leo Rosten, "The Intellectual and the Mass Media," *Daedalus* (Spring, 1960), pp. 33-46.

ity" to compiling rationales for conformity and to formulating schemes for better (therefore more "responsible") collective action.

The Intellectual, of course, does not *have* to escape into a private or inauthentic world of his own; he can become existential; he can be committed; he can keep pushing, learning, discussing, writing and acting—tuning in to important dialogue everywhere. He does not need to cease caring, thinking, agitating, taking serious things seriously; but it is a temptation, for being a "thinker" he realizes the growing insignificance of the individual person and the deterministic tendencies of a mass society.

The existentialist position insists that the journalist involve himself, commit himself, ever moving, ever changing—in short, he must continue to make or create himself. "Man is nothing else but what he makes of himself," Sartre has said, calling this the first principle of existentialism.[8] Certainly the existential journalist, in the serious business of making himself, would not be devoid of rationality, nor would he be a complete foe of Reason. Again, it is a matter of emphasis: the existential journalist would stress intuition, feeling and any other aspect of subjectivism which might help him acquire a more complete and realistic picture of the event or personality he is describing.

Existentialism does not exclude rationalism, but it does give significant emphasis to emotional and intuitive concerns. It also gives extraordinary attention to personal freedom—including the freedom to react emotionally or instinctively to one's environment. As Hazel Barnes says, the existentialist's "one certainty is his own freedom."[9] The existentialist believes that one cannot be ethical in his actions unless he is free; ethics implies freedom. I *ought* implies I *can*—that I have a choice. Therefore, it is easy to see why existentialists believe that B. F. Skinner and other determinists are "beyond ethics" since they believe that people are enslaved to forces over which they have no control, forces which cause them to act in certain ways regardless of their desires.

The Rationalist, in contrast to the existentialist, has a ten-

---

[8] Jean-Paul Sartre, *Existentialism and Human Emotions* (New York: Philosophical Library, 1957), p. 15.

[9] *An Existentialist Ethics* (New York: Random House—Vintage Books, 1971), p. 51.

dency to be more the scientist than the artist, the prosaic man than the poet, the Platonist than the Romantic, the Apollonian than the Dionysian. William Barrett has compared him to Jonathan Swift's "Laputans" in *Gulliver's Travels*.[10] He would be one of the cerebral people, powerful but dreary, and scientifically oriented. And, as Barrett says, the whole Romantic movement was an attempt to escape from Laputa—a protest of feeling against reason. This Romantic protest was furthered by the early existentialists such as Kierkegaard, who maintained that "it was intelligence and nothing else that had to be opposed." But Kierkegaard did not disparage intelligence; in fact he speaks of it with great respect. But he did believe it needed opposition with all the resources and intelligence at his disosal. It is significant that Kierkegaard called himself the "subjective thinker."[11] It is this "subjective thinking"—a sort of harmonious marriage of emotion and intelligence—that marks the existentialist in journalism and differentiates him from the Rationalist in journalism who is determined to exclude judgment and emotion from his work and make his every decision—ethical and otherwise—on the basis of Reason, and Reason alone.

The Two Basic Journalistic Tendencies

Out of all the various stances discussed above, two basic journalistic tendencies emerge. One of these is what might be referred to as a "subjective" orientation or tendency and the other as an "objective" tendency. The first is a tendency toward involvement and the second is a tendency toward aloofness. The first is more "sense-oriented" and the second is more "fact-oriented." The journalist with the "objective" tendency might be said to be more scientific than the "subjectivist," who is more artistic.

Although every journalist is, indeed, schizophrenic to some degree in respect to these two tendencies, my experience with journalism students and practicing journalists for some twenty-five years convinces me that every person in journalism evidences significantly more of one of these tendencies than of the other. An interesting hypothesis presents itself—one which I

---

[10] William Barrett, *Irrational Man* (New York: A Doubleday Anchor Book, 1962), pp. 122-23.

[11] *Ibid.*, p. 150.

believe is valid, but which has never really been tested: that journalists with the aloof, scientific or disinterested orientation are those whose pre-journalism education and interests were more "prosaic" than "poetic," more "scientific" than "artistic." And, on the other hand, the so-called "subjective" or involved journalists are persons with a pre-journalism background showing an inclination toward imaginative literature, philosophy and the humanities generally. It is also probably true that the "subjectivists" are more emotional, more sensitive, more convinced of their own rightness, more desirous to proselytize and propagandize, and more dogmatic than are the so-called "objectivists" or uninvolved journalists.

If the two orientations were to be summarized in terms of the various dichotomous tendencies discussed earlier, here is the way each would look:

• *The Existential (involved or artistic) Stance*—romantic, poetic, Dionysian, mystical, intuitive, emotional, subjective, personal, informal, directive, persuasive, humanistic, judgmental, liberal.

• *The Rationalist (aloof or scientific) Stance*—neutralist, Platonist and Apollonian, prosaic, objectivist, impersonal, formal, reportive, disinterested, non-judgmental, calm, unemotional, conservative.

Institutionalized journalism, or what might be called "Establishment Journalism" in the United States, has championed the second of these basic tendencies. Journalism schools and departments give significantly more emphasis to it than to the more subjective orientation. The underground journalistic movement of the 1960's, coupled with the resurrection of subjective "New" journalism[12] by such writers as Wolfe, Mailer, and Capote, made a noticeable dent (at least temporarily) in the aloof or scientific orientation, but news media and programs in journalism education still give short shrift to judgmental, involved, intuitive journalistic subjectivism.

There is still an overriding conviction in journalism that reporters should keep their opinions and biases out of their

---

[12] An excellent discourse on "new journalism," readable and brief is a monograph, *The New Journalism: A Critical Perspective* (Association for Education in Journalism, 1974). One of the most stinging criticisms of "new" journalism is found (pp. 440-41) in John Tebbel, *The Media in America* (New York: New American Library Mentor Books, 1974).

Basic Journalistic Orientations

STANCE	STANCE
Involved	Aloof
Romantic	Realistic
Poetic	Prosaic
Artistic	Scientific
Subjective	Objective
Personal	Impersonal
Passionate	Dispassionate
Informal	Formal
Directive	Imitative
Warm	Cold
Opinionated	Non-opinionated
Judgmental	Non-judgmental
Liberal	Conservative
Committed	Neutral
Dionysian	Apollonian
Intuitive	Logical
Personalistic	Factualistic
Non-conformist	Conformist
Unpredictable	Predictable
Flexible	Standardized

VALUES	VALUES
Freedom	Responsibility
Instability	Stability
Pluralism	Monism
Diversity	Sameness
Experimentation	Consistency
Change	Changelessness
Future	Past/Present
Spontaneity	Predictability
Egoism	Altruism
Individualism	Collectivism
Creativity	Conformity
Self-reliance	Dependence
Autonomy	Institutionalism
Emotions	Reason
Will	Determinism
Rebellion	Conformity

EXISTENTIALIST

RATIONALIST

stories and that subjective pieces and commentary be separated from news stories and be clearly identified. Those who are in favor of "integrated" journalism—in the sense of combining the reporter's judgments and opinions with the verifiable facts—are very much in the minority and are felt to be the eccentrics of modern American journalism. More about this will be presented later (in Chapter 5).

In spite of this "objectivist" leaning in American journalism, various existentialist voices do caution against it. Karl Jaspers notes that we need a great dissatisfaction "with what is merely correct," and that truth is "infinitely *more* than scientific correctness."[13] Hwa Yol Jung states that "the affirmation of objectivism to the exclusion of subjectivity is misleading because it ignores the place of subjectivity in thought and observation."[14] He continues:

> What is observable (a datum), for example, is always related to the awareness of an observer. A datum of observation is not yet a fact, and a fact is meaningful only in relation to the observer for whom it is a fact. Thus a fact is nothing but meaning given to a datum (or data) by the observer in the process of observation. Further, the truth of a fact or thought for one observer is sanctioned intersubjectively—that is, by a scientific or intellectual community. As consciousness is intentional, reflective thought, whether philosophical or scientific, is neither entirely subjective nor entirely objective.

Back in the 1940's the noted journalist, H. L. Mencken, put it more bluntly: "We talk of objective reporting. There is no such thing. I have been a reporter for many years, and I can tell you that no reporter worth a hoot ever wrote a purely objective story. You get a point of view in it. . . . You can't escape it. A man that is worth reading at all has opinions. He has ideas. And you are not going to improve him by trying to choke him."[15]

Journalism has been largely one-dimensional for many years. Even in more advanced countries journalism has been thought to be pretty simple: just give the facts in order of their importance.

---

[13]"Existenzphilosophie" in Walter Kaufmann (ed.), *Existentialism from Dostoevsky to Sartre* (New York: New American Library—Meridian Books, 1975), p. 175.

[14] In Hwa Yol Jung (ed.), *Existential Phenomenology and Political Theory: A Reader* (Chicago: Henry Regnery Co., 1972), xxvi.

[15] In Theo Lippman, Jr. (ed.), *A Gang of Pecksniffs* (New Rochelle, NY.: Arlington House, 1975), p. 203.

Oversimplifcation is, to a great extent, still the rule. The journalist has, at least in the United States, been conceived of as somebody who, either because of an ability or desire to write or a penchant for prying open doors of secrecy, gravitated to a journalistic position. Or, he was a political agitator who landed in journalism instead of politics. Generally, the journalist has been an uninvolved, reportorial type who has been nurtured in an atmosphere of the "objective" school of journalism which prizes the neutral stance. Occasionally, however, a Tom Wicker or a Daniel Schorr will break through—evidencing an existential emphasis. But this does not happen very often, and when it does even the "professional colleagues" tend to make such a stance uncomfortable.

What are the main characteristics of the "existential journalist" and how can he function in today's highly institutionalized and professionalized journalism? The broad outlines of this existential journalism is the subject of the next chapter.

Existential Journalism:
Outlines

The journalist . . . can merge himself in the tension and the reality of the day. . . . He can seek out that innermost region where the soul of the age takes a step forward. He deliberately interweaves his destiny with that of the epoch. He takes alarm, he suffers, and he balks when he encounters Nothingness. He becomes insincere when he is content with that which brings satisfaction to the majority. He soars towards the heights when he sincerely fulfills his being in the present.

—KARL JASPERS, *Man in the Modern Age*

The press must be a vital participant in public affairs, and an open and bold participant . . . unashamed of the fact that it is accepting a responsibility for playing such a role. . . . and it must not depend on the safe and stifling rules of some false objectivity, but depend upon the talent, the knowledge, the experience, the courage, and, above all, the individuality of the people who work in the press.

—TOM WICKER, *The Quill*

EXISTENTIAL JOURNALISM is a kind of synthesis of the attitudes expressed above in the quotations from a philosopher and a journalist. Unfortunately, the term is too often denuded of its vital meaning by being considered, when it is considered at all, as something nearly synonymous with "New Journalism." Actually it is different; for it is not simply an attitude or stance of rebellion for rebellion's sake, nor is it an obsession with writing style or form, nor is it a concern for exhaustive communication. Rather, existential journalism is that aspect of journalism mainly manifested in an attitude of freedom, commitment, rebellion, and responsibility. It makes no *a priori* assumptions as to the direction the journalism should take. It is mainly an orientation of being "true to one's self," however trite this may sound. So we can say that existential journalism is not the same as New Journalism, although they do have certain characteristics in common.

New Journalism, in its generalized meaning, is mainly concerned with form and style—or with an anti-establishment bias predominantly, or with confronting public taste through the use of four-letter words and unorthodox ideas, subjects, and pictures. It does often resemble existential journalism in that there is an inclination to rebel against conformity and authoritarian tendencies. However, it has been my observation that the so-called "New Journalists" are mainly "literary figures" who want a continuous forum, or they are counter-culture types who desire to shock the sensitivities of the general public. Often they are not really authentic and individualistic: they conform to their "own crowd" and the dictates of "their" philosophy or ideology; they do what seems to be currently in vogue with the rebels. In a sense, their guiding motto seems to be "Nonconformists of the World, Unite!" This is definitely *not* the stance of the existential journalist.

Some General Characteristics

Existential journalism is mainly a *subjective* journalism—subjective in the sense that it puts special stress on the *person* of the journalist himself. Certainly, I am not talking of an extreme subjectivism; rather the kind of existential journalism that is realistic and meaningful is a modified subjective journalism. It is mainly subjective, personal, and passionate; but at the same time it has a firm foundation of reasonableness. And, of course, reasonableness impinges on journalistic freedom, limiting it by *self*-assertion, making it "responsible" freedom. Therefore, when I use the term *existential* journalism, I am referring to this modified or nonextreme journalistic stance of existentialism.

In journalism, we normally repress the sense of subjectivity. We fail to recognize its inevitability as well as its pitfalls, its mystery, and its sober source of strength. Man is subjective. He cannot escape from himself—nor should he attempt it. When he tries to be objective—a "reflector" of his environment—he takes on a false nature; he becomes inauthentic. Freud has said that a person has an unconscious that motivates and influences his conscious choice of words and messages. The existentialist in journalism would agree with this, but it does indeed pose the problem of a kind of neutralist objectivity. Erich Fromm insists that "objectivity does not mean detachment, it means respect; that is, the ability not to distort and to falsify things, persons, and oneself."[1] Very often the journalist will adopt a stance of detachment, of disinterest; he is attempting to be true to what he calls "objectivity." Fromm takes issue with such a stance, and says that the idea that "lack of interest is a condition for recognizing the truth is fallacious."[2]

Existentialism is a philosophy of the subject rather than of the object; this, of course, shifts the emphasis for the existential journalist from an obsession with the "thing" or "person" he is writing about to his (the writer's) *perception* of what is being reported. The subject is the initiator of action and the center of feeling: this *subject* is the journalist. John Macquarrie points out that often such a style of philosophizing appears to be anti-intellectualist. The existentialist thinks passionately, Macquarrie says, "as one who is involved in the actualities of existence." Probably the existentialist who took an extreme position in favor of "feeling" *vis-à-vis* "the rational man" was Miguel de Un-amuno. Even though some other existentialists have paid more respect (especially Karl Jaspers) to reason than did Unamuno, it is still true that they all claim to found their philosophy on a broad non-rational basis and eschew any narrow intellectualism.[3]

Jean Wahl in his 1949 brief discussion of existentialism defines the existent individual (drawing on Kierkegaard) as one (a) who has an infinite interest in himself and his destiny, (b) always feels himself to be in the process of becoming, with a task before him, and (c) is impassioned, is inspired with what Kierkegaard calls "the passion of freedom."[4] Wahl also quotes

---

[1] Erich Fromm, *Man for Himself* (Greenwich, Conn.: A Fawcett Premier Book, 1966), p. 111.

[2] *Ibid.*, A good discussion of this point can be found in Karl Mannheim, *Ideology and Utopia* (New York: Harcourt, Brace and Co., 1936).

[3] John Macquarrie, *Existentialism* (Baltimore: Penguin Books, Inc., 1973), pp. 2-3.

[4] Jean Wahl, *A Short History of Existentialism* (New York: Philosophical Library, 1949), p. 4.

Heidegger as insisting that a person must constantly be moving upward and forward ("transcending Nothingness") towards (1) the world, (2) other persons, and (3) the future. "Therefore," he writes, "each of us is always in front of himself . . . constantly oriented toward his possibilities."[5] Increasingly, according to Heidegger, persons are living at the inauthentic level of Being; this, he says, is largely due to mass society "in which individuals are prepared to lead average and secure lives, left without major decisions, undisturbed and even protected by society in return for their specific services and functions predetermined by the managers of mass society."[6]

Existential journalism is future-oriented journalism. The existential journalist looks ever ahead, even when he writes of past (and "so-called present") events. In so looking, he takes upon himself what William Barrett has called "the burden of the past (or of what out of the past he selects as his inheritance)" and thereby "orients himself in a certain way to his present and actual situation in life."[7]

Existentialists make much of the thesis that existence precedes essence; in other words, a person makes himself what he is; his individual essence or nature develops out of his existence. He has no fixed essence handed him at birth; rather, he fabricates his own nature out of his freedom and the historical situation in which he lives. So, he must be future-oriented; he must project himself forward, using his freedom to make decisions and to live authentically. Sartre puts the idea in these words: "We mean that man first of all exists, encounters himself, surges up in the world—and defines himself afterwards." Sartre continues in his essay, "Existentialism is a Humanism," to say that man is really indefinable, and this is because to begin with he is nothing. "He will not be anything," Sartre states, "until later, and then he will be what he makes of himself."[8]

Rollo May has provided a brief and succinct statement on the character and importance of existentialism. This quotation, I think, provides the main foundation of existentialism upon which a philosophy of journalism can be built:

[5] *Ibid.*, p. 16.

[6] Hanno Hardt, "The Dilemma of Mass Communication: An Existential Point of View," *Philosophy & Rhetoric* (Penn State University), Vol. 5, No. 3.

[7] *Irrational Man: A Study in Existential Philosophy* (New York: Doubleday Anchor Books, 1962), p. 228.

[8] Quoted in Macquarrie, *op. cit.*, p. 3.

The protest of the existentialists was violent and at times desper-
ate (as in Nietzsche), at other times noble and courageous (as in
the resistance movement of Camus and Sartre), even if it seemed
to many observers to be ineffectual against the on-moving lava of
conformity, collectivism, and the robot man. The existentialists'
central proclamation was this: No matter how great the forces
victimizing the human being, man has the capacity to *know* that
he is being victimized, and thus to influence in some way how he
will relate *to* his fate. There is never lost that kernel of the power
to take some stand, to make some decision, no matter how
minute. This is why the existentialists hold that man's existence
consists, in the last analysis, of his freedom. Tillich has phrased
this view beautifully, "Man becomes truly human only at the
moment of decision."[9]

Taking into consideration the general principles of existentialism summarized above, I think we can say that existential
journalism:

● emphasizes that the existential journalist is a free and
authentic person, not simply a cog in the impersonal wheel of
journalism; that he is not replaceable or expendable;

● brings into sharp relief the uniqueness of every journalist's
individual existence and personality;

● causes practitioners to develop their integrity and individual personalities and to project their personalities into society
through their journalism;

● makes them rebel against being lost, anonymous
functionaries in journalism;

● extols freedom and responsibility for decisions in a day
when more and more people are trying to escape freedom and
journalists are ever more cheerfully disappearing into the reces-
ses of highly institutionalized "corporate" journalism. (The existential journalist may rebel against this trend toward corporate
journalism, but he is in for a hard fight, for the growth of
totalitarian regimes and the steady drift toward collective, paternalistic societies is testimony to the desire to "escape from
freedom" which Erich Fromm has written about so perceptive-
ly.)

Also, we can say that the existential journalist wants to
practice a journalism that means that he:

1) takes a certain viewpoint, a certain position, a certain

---

[9] As quoted in Raymond Van Over (ed.), *The Psychology of Freedom*
(Greenwich, Conn.: Fawcett Premier Books, 1974), p. 344.

stand, and ceases what may be called the "objective-neutralism" fallacy;

2) considers alternatives of action and makes a commitment to one or some, not resting on the comfortable assumption that a little of everything ranged rather equally is the best, the fairest, truest, and most objective journalism;

3) makes no hestitation in choosing, selecting, making decisions as to editorial determinations; the journalist insists on persistent choices, hard ones as well as easy ones. (The journalist knows that in a very true sense in journalism *when he chooses for himself, he chooses for all*. He, in effect, universalizes his choices; he determines for all what is "news" for him. He structures the world for others while structuring his own world in words and pictures.)

4) considers consequences of journalistic action and takes responsibility for it, not "passing the buck" or "copping out" by offering excuses or saying that he is simply following orders of a superior. (For the existential journalist there is no "superior" so far as decision-making or ethical stand is concerned. The journalist *is his own standard*; there is no other.)

5) accepts and *uses* freedom—personal and journalistic. He is dedicated to freedom; it is his imperative, and as an existentialist he sees *his* freedom as everyone's. He chooses freedom and, in so doing, he chooses freedom as desirable for everyone, thus adding a kind of Kantian dimension to his journalistic foundation. What he wills for himself, he wills for everyone. And in the case of freedom, this is a highly dangerous and often uncomfortable position since the freedom of others may often cause actions not in keeping with one's own values or interests.

6) is vital, dynamic, passionate, and committed. (The existential journalist is repelled by stagnant, conformist, routine, uncommitted, dispassionate journalism—journalism that enshrines harmony, stability, safety, and complacency. The existential journalist wants to practice vigorous, dangerous journalism. It is through such a practice that he really *exists* as a journalist; thus he makes himself constantly into a journalist who is authentic; it is in this way that he creates his own journalistic essence, that he becomes more than a piece of machinery in the newsroom.)

7) extols individualism. (This means that he looks on the world and journalistic issues from *his* personal viewpoint. It means that how he looks on the world as a reporter *is* the world;

and as a reporter he transmits at least a portion of his total perceptions to his reader as *his world.)*

Freedom: The Existentialist's Imperative

What a journalist does in specific cases does not matter as much as the fact that he *does something*. The supreme virtue for the existentialist is probably the most old-fashioned of all: *integrity*. And a person cannot have integrity unless he utilizes his capacity to choose, to act, to make decisions. Basic to man is this act of choosing; the existentialist sees man's very nature consisting of choosing. And this choosing is an outgrowth of freedom; or, said another way, it can have real meaning only in an atmosphere of freedom. To the question, "What good is life?" comes the answer: Life in the abstract is worthless. As a person lives his life, its value can be judged by what he puts into it. Values are a projection of man's personal freedom. For the existentialist man *is* freedom; he does not possess freedom. Freedom, for the existentialist, comes as close as possible to constituting man's very essence. Man's most basic desire is for independent, free choice—at least, this is *existential* man's most basic desire.

Responsibility, for the existentialist, is seen as freedom's anchorage. Man is responsible for himself, of course, but also for each act, and for the consequences of each act. Nobody else can be responsible for what a person is; each person must act freely and accept the responsibility for his action. And to choose for oneself is to choose for others. What would others do in my place? Strangely, perhaps, existentialists view this universalized personal choice in much the same way as the coldly formal Kant did: You must never will what you cannot consistently will should be willed by other rational (i.e., free and responsible) beings. This heavy sense of personal responsibility the existentialists call "anguish." Sartre has said that man is "condemned" to be free, and Kierkegaard wrote of the necessity to choose only "in fear and trembling." But choose we must—for ourselves and for all others, with no final assurance that our choice is the "right" one.[10].

---

[10] Abraham Kaplan, *The New World of Philosophy* (New York: Vintage Books, 1961), pp. 97-128.

Naturally we attempt to escape the implications of this existential situation. Lama Anagarika Govinda has written that "generally we live away from life, either by being occupied with the past, or by anticipating the future."[11] Only while living "in the present, i.e., in moments of full awareness and 'awakedness,' are we free," she added.[12] Often we try to escape our present— and thus ourselves; we try to deny that we are responsible for our actions by denying that we are free. This is "bad faith." The journalist, for example, may often say that *he* would not have written the story in such a way—or would not have written it at all—but that he "had to do it" because he was told by his editor. He is thereby denying his freedom and refusing to accept personal responsibility for his actions. In practical terms, this embrace of "determinism" in various of its forms, amounts to denying that we are to blame for our actions—or for our morality. Existentialists, enshrining freedom, have no sympathy for these deterministic philosophies. And people who accept them, who try to escape the human condition of freedom and personal responsibility, are seen as cowards. The existentialist realizes that man must accept unquestioned responsibility for his ethical choices and actions. Man is an individualist: he is the end-all and the be-all of values. If the journalist is free he is, in a sense, condemned to live with his freedom—condemned to live with uncertainty and shifting situations in which he must constantly fashion his own standards. This is a terrifying, uncertain experience, filled with anguish; but it is the key to authentic essence-building existence.

Self-deception, for the existentialist, is the greatest vice, for it robs man of his personhood, his integrity; it deludes him into thinking that he is nothing more than a robot having an essence pushed upon him by *outside* forces. Man *makes himself*, says the existentialist, or defines what he is in the course of choosing, acting and existing.

The philosophical strain of freedom is basic to a sound and authentic journalistic orientation. Existentialism stresses this freedom; so does Kant, actually, but there is a difference. Sartre agrees with Kant in conceiving of freedom as "desiring both itself and the freedom of others." But, Sartre notes, Kant believes

---

[11] Quoted in Van Over (ed.), *The Psychology of Freedom*, p. 248.
[12]*Ibid*., p. 249.

that "the formal and universal are enough to constitute an ethics"; existentialists, on the other hand, "think that principles which are too abstract run aground in trying to decide action."[13] Sartre emphasizes personal responsibility—absolute responsibility for actions taken in specific cases and considering specific circumstances. So we can say that the existentialist, although prizing freedom, is basically a situationist while Kant is a universalist.

Action implies freedom. Since existentialists advocate action, they would, of course, place freedom near to the heart of their philosophy. They have a passion for freedom; this is true of all varieties of existentialists. Freedom for the existentialist is a basic postulate for action; it is already present as a condition for human existence. Freedom, of course, is dangerous; it even tends to contain in itself the seed of its own destruction. Nikolai Berdyaev, an existentialist who has written much on the subject of freedom, puts it this way: "The tragedy of the world process is that of freedom; it is born of the inner dynamic of freedom, of its capacity for changing into its opposite."[14] In striking this note, Berdyaev is consistent with many of his fellow existentialists. Plato, although not an existentialist, had, in his classic "Paradox of Freedom," pre-dated the existentialists in pointing out this danger centuries earlier when he noted that free men could freely decide to become enslaved.

Freedom may indeed be dangerous. And for many it is uncomfortable; they constantly attempt to escape from it and live inauthentic lives—"in bad faith." Nevertheless, freedom is absolutely necessary to an open society, to a democracy, to a libertarian people—and certainly to a pluralistic and diversified journalism. And, as existentialists contend, there is no human dignity without freedom—and "the risk of increasing freedom must constantly be taken," as John Macquarrie puts it.[15] Existentialists generally link freedom with creativity. Without freedom *from* restraints, man cannot have freedom *for* creative activity. Berdyaev and other existentialists reveal a certain elitist or aristocratic tendency; the masses, they say, do not really value freedom and are satisfied with the routine daily existence. For this reason

---

[13] Jean-Paul Sartre, *Existentialism and Human Emotions* (New York: Philosophical Library—The Wisdom Library, 1957), p. 47.

[14] Macquarrie, *op. cit.*, p. 140.

[15] *Ibid.*, p. 141.

the masses "are peculiarly exposed to the dangers of dictator-
ship, founded on demagogy."[16] This is undoubtedly true, for it is
the rebel against the tryannizing and conforming influences of
the masses who cherishes freedom; it is he who protests against
every attempt to diminish freedom. It is he who realizes, as did
Albert Camus, that "freedom preserves the power to protest and
guarantees human communication."[17]

The freedom-loving journalist can find perhaps his greatest
support from the existentialists, for here is a philosophy which
rebels against any social control system which tends to enslave
the individual human being and to lead to his depersonalization.
Frederick Patka writes that existentialists "protest against this
total subjection of the individual by the organized many" and
that they "demand a bold revolt against this state of affairs with a
view to the emancipation and autonomy of the individual person."[18]

The modern journalist, within whom the potent existentialist
freedom is strong, will recognize the potential danger of manipu-
lating and enslaving others. If he desires freedom for himself, he
will desire it for others and he will cherish their authenticity and
autonomy as he cherishes his own. The real freedom-lover, in
other words, will defend freedom for others as well as for
himself. He knows full well that when only *some* have freedom,
they are tyrants and autocrats—or at least they have the potential
within them to be. When *all* have freedom, at least everyone has
the power to counteract tyranny and autocracy—or to escape
from it through his own freedom. The existential journalist is
certainly free to exercise his freedom in ways considered irresponsible to others, but the strain of Kantian morality and the
humanist in him will temper his activities with moderation,
concern, and *self*-responsibility and will keep him from falling
into the abyss of nihilism.

The existential spirit is especially important for the journalist
for it provides the fundamental foundation of his creative activity; it spurs him to action, to commitment and a determination to
launch out into new journalistic regions. What he *does* makes

---

[16] *Ibid.*

[17] Albert Camus, *The Rebel* (New York: Alfred Knopf, Inc. and Random
House—Vintage Books, 1954), p. 291.

[18] Frederick Patka in F. Patka (ed.), *Existentialist Thinkers and Thought*
(New York: The Citadel Press, 1966), pp. 42-43.

him authentic, real, human. How he reacts to his world through his journalism defines him as a journalist. *"Respondeo, ergo sum."*[19]

Journalists must respond to their environment—to their own journalistic situation. They are more than neutral observers; if they are not, then they are *nothing*. The true existentialist in journalism gets *into* the story, becomes part of the story. His perceptions, his sensitivity to the stimuli of the story infiltrates the story; in short, the existential journalist is part of the story and the story is part of him. This, of course, affects the journalistic Self and disrupts any demeanor of "objective neutralism"; it brings subjectivity to bear on the Event-Reporter-Report nexus, and it is what largely injects journalism with Dionysian ingredients of artistry, sensitivity, emotionalism, personalism, mysticism, opinionism, and creativity.

The Existential Journalist

Tom Wicker is one journalist on the contemporary scene who has challenged the news media to analyze themselves and get rid of the old notions of "objectivity" and "noninvolvement" which have all but been considered sacred in this century. The associate editor of *The New York Times* told a journalism group in 1975 that he saw the possibility for a "new age of the press" in America, a press which he characterized as "intellectual in the fundamental direction . . . challenging to all institutions of power . . . analytical in its general approach . . . involved in what is happening in our country."[20]

Since there are not many Wickers around today, it is good to have his hopeful words, indicating that existential journalism may be just around the corner. While I admire Wicker and applaud the substance of his optimism, I expect that it reflects mainly his "hopes" and the natural rhetoric of a person talking to journalists at a conference. If pessimism is characteristic of an existentialist, then, at least in this one respect, I am more existential than is Wicker. I do not see this American journalism in which the journalist will be "an open and bold participant" as

---

[19] See Ch. 12 ("Respondeo ergo Sum") in F. H. Heinemann, *Existentialism and the Modern Predicament* (New York: Harper Torchbooks, 1958), pp. 190-204.

[20] "Let's stop playing it safe," *The Quill* (December, 1975), p. 15.

imminent—or even possible in the long-run in this country. Timidity in journalism is being born; conformity and complacency are just now settling in. Increasing pressures from minority groups, government, the legal profession, and even from cautious and weak-kneed journalists themselves are killing any upsurge of existential journalism.

Journalism history can point to Addison, Steele, and Swift; it can single out Thomas Paine and Henry Thoreau; it can make a gesture toward I. F. Stone and Hodding Carter; and it can nod casually at Ernest Hemingway and H. L. Mencken; it can point to European "literary" journalists such as J.-P. Sartre and Albert Camus, and it can cast a cautious reference to Dan Rather, Tom Wicker, and Daniel Schorr. Journalism history can, indeed, dredge up some notable examples of existential journalists—but not very many.

Now, this is not to say that there have not been very many. But, generally, they are not the "big names" that burst forth into history or the public view; they are the pushers, tuggers, rebels, and involvers that go about their daily existential labors without benefit of national forum in the big newspapers, magazines, or broadcasting networks. A close study of the daily journalistic endeavors of individual journalists in the country would undoubtedly uncover a considerable number of existentialists. But they are not the wave of the future; in fact, there is no doubt but that they are being penalized at present, and in the future they will have no status or state in the increasingly timid, conformist, and corporate journalism.

A good example (perhaps the best) of an existential journalist is Albert Camus, who died in 1960. In 1943 he joined the underground group called "Combat," struggling against Nazi occupation of France. For this group, Camus edited a newspaper called *Combat*. The hundreds of articles he wrote for this paper make a record of the reactions of this sensitive, intelligent, and combative individual and provide an extended profile of an existentialist in journalism. During the black days of World War II, *Combat* was, for thousands of Frenchmen, a source of information, of stimulation, of pride, of hope and comfort. After the liberation of Paris (August, 1944), Camus continued his association with journalism by writing regularly for the weekly serious paper of Paris, *L'Express* (now a magazine). He also contributed articles to many French newspapers, doing so until the time of his death in an automobile accident in 1960.

Camus defined a good journalist as one who had a passionate concern and respect for himself, for others, and for truth. He believed that a good journalist was one "who, first of all, is supposed to have ideas."[21] In addition, Camus believed that the good journalist's task "is to inform the public on events which have just taken place," since "he is a sort of day-to-day historian whose prime concern is the truth." He elaborated on this, however, by saying that the "first news" is not always the best news and that "it is better to come in second and report the truth than to be first and false."[22]

Camus evidenced in his journalism (and in his novels and short stories) a depth and maturity indicative of existentialism. He treasured the rebel, to be sure, but he realized that freedom and rebellion implies responsibility. Maturity demands realism, and for Camus, realism led to the virtues of moderation. It was his belief that every individual must seek the measure, the harmony, the order, which will ensure his own freedom and integrity, and—equally important—the freedom and integrity of all others.

Without a doubt Camus was an existential journalist; he was other things, too, of course, but the *journalist* was very strong in him. But, in spite of this fact, Camus did not have much faith in journalism generally, considering it to be, by and large, superficial, careless, pedestrian, and vulgar. He seemed to realize that most journalists were non-existential, that they had no real desire to dig deeply into reality, to commit themselves to truth, to take unpopular positions, and to fight against the enslavements of mass society. In short, Camus saw the press situation as dismal. So had José Ortega y Gasset, the notable Spanish philosopher, who, too, had dabbled in journalism from time to time.

Ortega has referred to the "emanations of the press" as being on a "very low spiritual plane."[23] He calls the typical journalist

[21] Jean Daniel, "Camus as Journalist," *New Republic* (June 13, 1964), p. 19. For further details on Camus as a journalist, see Germaine Brée, *Camus and Sartre: Crisis and Commitment* (New York: Dell Publishing Co.—A Delta Book, 1972), pp. 36, 52, 203, 214, 245, and 249.

[22] Daniel, *op. cit.*

[23] *Mission of the University* (New York: W. W. Norton & Co.,—The Norton Library, 1944), p. 90.

"one of the least cultured types in contemporary society," and one that deforms reality when he "reduces the present to the momentary, and the momentary to the sensational."[24] It is obvious that Ortega did not think too highly of journalism, although its role in society was considered to be very important.

Karl Jaspers, too, was of somewhat the same mind about journalism. While recognizing the importance of the press in bringing "into the consciousness of the times what otherwise would remain the ineffective possession of a few individuals,"[25] he admits that it is extremely difficult to find a "terse and highly polished insight . . . amid the multifarious rubbish of what is printed from day to day."[26]

One of today's broadcast journalism reporters, Charles Kuralt, believes a great segment of news is being overlooked by the press. "There is much in our country to be confident and reassured about," he says, "but confidence and reassurance are not the province of the front page or the evening news."[27] Kuralt suggests that journalists could do more than merely inform people; "We may help educate them occasionally," he writes. "We may help broaden their vision and elevate their spirits. We may accept the responsibility we have to be better than we are, broader than we are, calmer and more reflective."[28] Jacques Ellul, a contemporary sociologist and social philosopher, agrees with Kuralt on his general view of journalism, saying that "the news is only about trouble, danger and problems."[29] This, he believes, is largely responsible for the anxiety that plagues individuals in today's society; he writes that

> . . . this gives man the notion that he lives in a terrible and frightening era, that he lives amid catastrophes in a world where everything threatens his safety. Man cannot stand this; he cannot live in an absurd and incoherent world (for this he would have to be heroic, and even Camus, who considered this the only honest posture, was not really able to stick to it); nor can he accept the idea that the problems, which sprout all around him, cannot be

[24] *Ibid.*

[25] Karl Jaspers, *Man in the Modern Age* (Garden City, N.Y.: Doubleday Anchor Books, 1957), p. 134.

[26] *Ibid.*, pp. 124-25.

[27] "Journalism is crisis-ridden; the country is not," *The Bulletin* of ASNE (Jan., 1976), p. 15.

[28] *Ibid.*

[29] Jacques Ellul, *Propaganda* (New York: Vintage Books, 1973), p. 146.

solved, or that he himself has no value as an individual and is subject to the turn of events. The man who keeps himself informed needs a framework in which all this information can be put in order; he needs explanations and comprehensive answers to general problems; he needs coherence. And he needs an affirmation of his own worth.

And then there is John Carroll, writing in New York's *The Village Voice* and criticizing the press coverage of Patty Hearst, before and during her trial:

> And so the crowds, the believers and the criers, the jailhouse johnnies and the electronic groupies fulfilled the media prophecy. They saw themselves in the funhouse media mirror. And they waved their arms at their own reflections, seeking fame by association, dancing jerkily on the outskirts of history. They came because the media said it was a big story; the media proved that it was a big story because the crowds came. It's like the old Gertrude Stein drinking song, "We're here because we're here because we're here because . . ."[30]

Now, back to Tom Wicker. He is one of my candidates for an outstanding existential journalist, but there are not many. He, too, attacks the press—but his stress is on the impulse of the press "to play it safe." Writing about the press and the Watergate Affair, Wicker says: "We'll never know how many things might have appeared, should have appeared, but did not appear because of that impulse of self-censorship on the part of the press, an impulse to play it safe."[31] According to Wicker, this tendency poses a great danger in journalism—perhaps the greatest—and editors, publishers, and reporters must constantly fight against it "with the greatest degree of alertness."[32] Wicker has consistently called for an existential stance in journalism; and his words have been clearer and more forceful in this regard than most journalists are prepared to accept.

It was to be expected that Wicker would be admonished for his existential position. An example of this was a letter in *The Quill* two months later,[33] most of which is quoted below:

---

[30] As reprinted in *The Bulletin* of ASNE (Jan., 1976), p. 15.

[31] *The Quill* (Dec. 1975), p. 16.

[32] *Ibid.*

[33] *The Quill* (Feb., 1976), p.4. The writer of the letter was B. R. Berry of Westerville, Ohio. His reaction probably reflects the opinion of the great majority of American journalists and journalism professors.

Wicker is suggesting the public be fed news oriented to advocate a particular point of view: "The press must above all be fair and accurate, but not necessarily be a press that is in the traditional sense of the word, objective and neurtral." The press as he sees it, would not depend greatly upon "the safe and stifling rules of some false objectivity, but depend upon the talent, knowledge, experience, courage, and above all, the individuality of the people who work in the press."

Do you really want the news people you know (or any other group for that matter) to have that much power and that little accountability? Such a position certainly is not in agreement with the new code of ethics just adopted by the American Society of Newspaper Editors. . . .

Wicker is afraid of playing it safe. I am afraid of irresponsibility. It can kill freedom of the press. There is no need for freedom of the press if it does not report the unbiased truth. Otherwise, we simply substitute one tyranny for another.

In February, 1976, Tom Wicker went out on a limb again— this time when he defended Daniel Schorr of CBS News. Not many other journalists of national reputation came to Schorr's defense; in fact, most were highly critical of the CBS reporter who made a copy of the House Intelligence Committee's report available for publication in *The Village Voice*, a New York weekly newspaper. CBS News had just suspended Schorr from his reporting duties for the action. Wicker was angry, and dealt with the subject in his column, syndicated by the New York Times Service and printed during the month by many newspapers. He began by saying that CBS News "had succumbed to a campaign launched within the Ford administration picturing the Central Intelligence Agency as an erring but basically worthy victim of those who leak its vital secrets and reporters who print them." Then he went on to give the history of the incident, and to relate it to the government charge about publication of the Pentagon Papers in 1971.

Wicker pointed a critical finger at the House of Representatives, and asked: "How is it different for the House to vote to suppress a public document than for a president to suppress it? If President Ford, for example, had decided not to make public the report of the Rockefeller Commission he appointed to study CIA abuses, would that have made it 'just plain wrong' for a good reporter like Dan Schorr to get hold of it and put it on the public record? Of course not." And, Wicker ended his column with a word of praise for Schorr: "After a year-long investigation conducted at public expense, it [the committee report] was in fact a document that belonged where Dan Schorr put—on the public record."

Harrison Salisbury, a former associate editor of *The New York Times* and the founder of its "op-ed" page, is another journalist I must mention here; for certainly he evidences flashes of the existential spirit. In an article in *The Columbia Journalism Review*,[34] Salisbury recounts how he ran into the conformist tendencies in the press (and the pressures from the White House and Pentagon) when he wrote a series of articles from Hanoi in late 1966 and early 1967. He also tells of correspondents in both the Korean and Vietnam wars who favored the imposition of censorship on their stories: "Apparently they thought censorship would remove the problem of confronting the moral issues of war reporting. Let the government decide what was right—or not right."[35] This, of course, would be a good example of Sartrean "bad faith"—a kind of escape from using freedom to make one's own choices and decisions.

Salisbury takes a definite existentialist position when he poses these questions about reporting: "Can we turn ourselves into computers? Should we try to divorce ourselves from the human race? Should we turn our backs on injustice? Why protect an objectivity which we do not and cannot possess? Would we all not be more honest—would not the reader be better served—if we carefully stated our prejudices and then did our best to tell the facts as we had discovered them to be?[36] *These are all important existential questions!* They, at least in large part, mark out some of the basic concerns of the existentialist in journalism. One's reaction to them, his attitude toward them, and his answers to them will serve to indicate whether or not he is existential or not in his basic journalistic stance.

A Few Concluding Remarks

Existential journalism begins with a kind of pessimism. Why? Because of a concern with death among existentialists generally, but in the case of journalism it is not so much the individual's

---

[34] *The Columbia Journalism Review* (Jan./Feb., 1976).
[35] *Ibid.*, p. 51.
[36] *Ibid.*, p. 53.

death, but the knowledge that press freedom is dying everywhere. It is disappearing rapidly. The journalism of the world is going toward authoritarianism everywhere. It is really the old process of entropy at work: the inclination of a system to run down, become passive. With such a recognition, the freedom-loving existential journalist naturally is anxious, develops a kind of *Angst*; but this anxiety does not debilitate the journalist—on the contrary, this very sense of the impending doom of journalistic freedom instills in him the desire to live fully his freedom while time remains.

The existential journalist has the conviction of the death of journalistic freedom; therefore, he must live every minute of every day in such a way as to maximize his own freedom and autonomy. He can thus create small "islands of decreasing entropy," as Norbert Wiener has put it.

This "sense of freedom's doom," this anxiety, leads to a concern for involvement, to a commitment to commitment. No more is the journalist satisfied to simply muddle through the day, doing the same old mechanistic duties, being caught in the ever-deepening rut in the newsroom. There is a new dedication to commitment, to making every day count, to pushing back the limits of restrictions, to suggesting the unorthodox, to daring to be honest—in short, to making oneself into an ever more authentic journalist and person.

Journalism is a way of life, and the journalist *exists* in this way. Acting journalistically is the main thing; having a theory about journalism is another, and of much lesser import. A code of ethics hanging on the wall is meaningless; a code of ethics internalized within the journalist and guiding his actions is what is meaningful. Action, really, and not theory is the thing that counts with the existentialist. Theory without action is dead. If all the "theory" and words about commitment and action which one hears at many journalism conventions were translated into action, there would truly be a revolution in the press. The freedom-loving, active, imaginative, and committed journalist is hard to find.

But, I can hear myriads of cautious organization-persons crying: Is there not a danger that existential journalists would pose problems for the viability and stability of the newspapers and other media? Wouldn't existential journalists go too far with this individualistic, creative urge? Wouldn't they go overboard and hurt the collective, corporate effort we're making?

My answer: Some of them well might. And, in many cases, it would be good if they did. We need a lot of fresh air blowing into most journalistic media. But, actually, there is nothing for the media managers and the conformist journalists to fear, for there is no serious danger from these existential journalists. They will simply not be numerous enough to pose any real danger to the ever-growing corporate structure of journalism.

I hope that this chapter has presented at least the main outlines of existential journalism in such a way that some clarification of the term has been made. Probably there are still many questions in the reader's mind as to just what existential journalism is. But at least a start has been made to explicate this journalistic orientation, and it is hoped that the chapters which follow will shed further light on the essential nature of existential journalism.

Pessimism, Anxiety, and Freedom

The Existentialist thinker feels solitary in the midst of today's society, cut off from nature, and the rest of humanity, his most intimate friends, and even his deepest self. This many-sided alienation weighs on him like an eternal fate that cannot be changed or conquered, even though man is obliged to contest against it.

—GEORGE NOVACK, *Existentialism versus Marxism*

Many young people, it is true, do not seem to value freedom. But some of us still believe that, without freedom, human beings cannot become fully human and that freedom is therefore supremely valuable. Perhaps the forces that now menace freedom are too strong to be resisted for very long. It is still our duty to do whatever we can to resist them.

—ALDOUS HUXLEY, *Brave New World Revisited*

TODAY'S JOURNALISTS, along with the rest of us, are caught up in something close to what the sociologists call *anomie*, the mechanistic and non-creative work that comprises our daily routine, a lack of fulfillment and isolation from a finished product, and the absence from participation in decision. This, the sociologists say, is at the root of a broad spiritual malaise; and this *anomie* certainly resembles the existentialists' concept of "alienation." It is the very *anomie*, say many sociologists, that works toward socialization, that leads persons to organize, to join, to lose themselves in a group or collectivity. This helps to wipe out the terrible feeling of alienation and personal anxiety. So, from one perspective, we can look on this feeling of alienation as a stimulus to socialization and a road to psychological comfort. Conforming and cooperating is, in a sense, a means of living harmoniously, not only with others but also with oneself.

This, however, is not the view of the existentialist. A person should *not* escape from the anxieties of life; he should not try to find safe havens of psychological conformity into which to flee from the violent storms of life. In fact, he should accept these buffetings, these feelings of alienation and anxiety as natural and necessary aspects of *true being*. The existentialist looks on this ontological anxiety as the catalyst to real *intensive* living. The journalist, for example, who escapes the vicissitudes of life through routinized and conformist journalism is, from an existentialist perspective, dead. He is "comfortable," perhaps, but his is the "comfort" of a stone or a tree. It is through striving, fighting, involving himself, suffering, and agonizing fully in the mainstream of life that he truly lives.

For the existentialist, the world is a rough and dangerous place; it is not to be fled and hidden from. It is to be faced squarely. The existentialist knows that dangers are all around him; it is this very recognition that causes him anxieties and anguish. He also knows that facing these dangers and living totally with the resulting anguish is what makes him truly a person and thrusts him into new and intensive levels of existence. He is not, like the utilitarian, seeking happiness; rather he is seeking total, true, *intensive* living.

Alienation in the Modern World

The journalist, at once isolated from society in his role as its reporter-interpreter and at the same time knowledgeable about the happenings of society, feels himself alienated. He lives in his own little verbal world of symbols abstracted from reality; he sees the world as scribbles on a page, images on a tube, or sounds from a speaker. He, in effect, tends to become a piece of transmitting machinery himself; he finds it difficult to retain his own personhood, his own identity, his own individuality as he routinely collects, packages, and transmits "the world" to others.

He almost becomes someone other than himself. Actually, as Jacques Ellul has pointed out, alienation largely means this very process: being someone other (*alienus*) than oneself. And, says Ellul, it also can mean to "belong to someone else," "to be deprived of one's self," "to be subjected to, or even identified with, someone else."[1] As the journalist *fits in* more and more snugly with his communication medium, he increasingly becomes "someone other" than himself; he belongs to *someone else* as he takes orders and ceases to exercise his own creativity. He is deprived of himself, detached from society (although he "reports" it), and lives in his own little world of corporate journalism in a passive, second-hand world created by himself and his colleagues.

Journalists, in their mainly neutralist, dispassionate role, become overly detached from society. They do, of course, come in contact with representatives of society, but mainly these persons are looked upon simply as "sources," as "participants," as "spokesmen"—in short, as *news*. According to Camus and other existentialists, this isolation of persons and groups from real life and vital society is growing; more and more, people in society are voluntarily and involuntarily being alienated. Perhaps Camus's novel *The Stranger* illustrates this isolation or estrangement as well as any literary work; it combines the issues of alienation, self-estrangement, the mechanization of the person and the general loss of true personhood.[2]

Robert Olson believes that, for the existentialist, the chief value in life is intensity—exemplified in acts of free choice, individual self-assertion, personal love, and creative work. And, says Olson, these various "forms of intensely lived experience are impossible without anguish, suffering, and risk."[3] One main cause of this suffering is what Olson calls the "anguish before the necessity of choosing"—what is often referred to as the "anguish of freedom." Erich Fromm deals with this in his *Escape from Freedom*, in which he observes that a man's loneliness is usually caused by freedom, and that when he achieves freedom, he tends to experience isolation, loneliness and even self-estrangement. So, with the existentialists, Fromm would say that a recognition (and use) of freedom is what brings about this alienation. In a later book, *The Revolution of Hope*, Fromm deals with ways

[1] Jacques Ellul, *Propaganda* (New York: Knopf—Vintage Books, 1973), p. 169.

[2] *The Stranger* (New York: Vintage Books, 1946).

[3] Robert G. Olson, *An Introduction to Existentialism* (New York: Dover Publications, Inc., 1962), p. 19.

technocracies aid in producing self-alienation and mechanization of action in human beings; he ties this trend to the decline of faith and the rise of scientism—the search for scientific truth. Modern man, according to Fromm, has concentrated on technical and material values and has lost the capacity for deep emotional experiences. The machines he has built, posits Fromm, have become so powerful that they have dehumanized him.[4]

Gabriel Marcel, the French Christian existentialist, also believes that technocracy—as well as large organizations—leads to this personal alienation of which Fromm speaks.[5] This impact of technology and organization will be taken up later in this chapter. Carl Jung places much of the blame for the estrangement—or as he puts it, "psychic isolation"—of the individual on the doorstep of the mass State. According to Jung, the State wants the person to be isolated, for "the more unrelated individuals are, the more consolidated the State becomes, and vice versa."[6]

Whatever the reasons for this alienation or estrangement, it is seen by existentialists as part of authentic living. It must be faced, and transcended by action; it must be overcome by an increased respect for Self. For, in effect, the existentialist considers alienation in chiefly inward terms; it is a person's alienation from his deepest being. As John Macquarrie says, an alienated person "is not himself but simply a cipher in the mass-existence of the crowd or a cog in the industrial system or whatever it may be."[7] The existentialist faces this alienation and turns it into a part of his true existence—a catalyst for intensive life. But we can see that mass society itself alienates—not only in separating persons from authentic relationships with others, but in separating them from their own true existence. Kierkegaard has stressed that man must function as an individual, but in meaningful relationship to other individuals, in order to overcome the corroding effects of alienation. He envisioned social man absorbed in a group or a crowd as "inhuman."[8]

---

[4] *The Revolution of Hope* (New York: Harper & Row, 1968), p. 2 ff.

[5] *Man Against Mass Society* (Chicago: Henry Regnery Co.—a Gateway Edition, 1969), p. 204.

[6] C. G. Jung, *The Undiscovered Self* (New York: Mentor Books, 1958), p. 115.

[7] *Existentialism* (New York: Penguin Books, 1973), p. 160.

[8] Nicholas A. Horvath, *Philosophy* (Woodbury, N.Y.: Barron's Educational Series Inc., 1974), p. 106.

Journalistic Anxiety and Anguish

Out of a background of alienation, anxiety and anguish—all really blending together like a black cloud over man—comes this pervading sense of pessimism that seems to mark all existentialists. Frustration, insecurity, and painful striving are the inescapable lot of mankind; however, some persons try to minimize this, try to escape from it, but the existentialist, as Robert Olson has said, looks on this dismal situation as something to be squarely faced: it is only in so confronting the pain and dangers of life that life is worth living. Olson adds that a life of frustration, insecurity, and anguish produces values, and "the values so generated are the only ones actually realizable and genuinely worthy of human pursuit."[9]

Meeting life squarely, loving the struggle, and avoiding any temptation to seek safety in seclusion: this is a main message of the existentialist. This refrain, with many variations, has been heard many times through the years. Listen to the words of Henry David Thoreau:

> However mean your life is, meet it and live; do not shun it and call it hard names. It is not so bad as you are. It looks poorest when you are richest. The fault-finder will find faults even in paradise. Love your life, poor as it is.[10]

What is this "anxiety" (or *Angst*) that encompasses the person? It is difficult to explain, for it is a feeling, a sense, a kind of dismal premonition. The existentialists seem to have in mind a subtle emotion of "uneasiness" or "malaise"; sometimes they use the terms "dread" and "anguish," but usually "anxiety" appears to be the best English word to describe it. Anxiety is linked to freedom, often described as the "vertigo" or "dizziness" of freedom.[11]

> Anxiety arises rather because "I distrust myself and my own reactions" (Sartre). In other words, there is a profound ambiguity in freedom—hence the paradoxical expression we are *condemned* to be free. A nothingness slips into my action. I am not the self that I will be, or I am it in the mode of not being it.[12]

---

[9] Olson, p. 14.

[10] *Thoreau on Man and Nature*, a compilation of writings of Thoreau by A. D. Volkman (Mt. Vernon, N.Y.: The Peter Pauper Press, 1960), p. 24.

[11] Macquarrie, p. 129.

[12] *Ibid*., p. 131.

This idea of not being what I will be, this idea of "nothing-ness" at the moment, is important to the existentialist, and, as Macquarrie points out above, is responsible for much of the anxiety which we have. The journalist is suspended, as it were, between two moments of nothingness; he senses that he is constantly headed toward the annihilation of his own contingency—*In der Welt zum Tode sein*, as Heidegger puts it. Frederick Patka interprets this in the following short passage:

> I am what I was, that is, nothing; I also am what I will be, that is, nothing again, for past and future as such are located outside the horizon of actuality. This experience of anguish and dread, conditioned by the awareness of one's complete contingency, is of the greatest value to the existentialists, for they believe that it is here at this crucial moment of personal crisis that the "opening for transcendence" emerges.[13]

Anxiety does not only arise from our recognition of freedom or from the sense of our constant hanging between two points of "nothingness"; it also tends to well up from within us as an "uncanny apprehension of some impending evil, of something not within us, but of an alien power."[14] And, for some, anxiety is seen as "despair" and despair is "the sickness unto death."[15] One type of anxiety is caused by "self-estrangement"—not external, but something going on in the person himself. Kier-kegaard heralded the Age of Anxiety; it is now full upon us.

Jacques Ellul says that anxiety (which he equates with psychological fear) is perhaps "the most widespread psychologi-cal trait in our society." Of course, says Ellul, we have good reasons to be afraid—"of Communist subversion, revolution, Fascism, H-bombs, conflict between East and West, unemploy-ment, sickness." He points out that on one hand the number of dangers is increasing, and the news media make us more aware of them, and on the other hand, religious beliefs, which allowed man to face fear, have almost disappeared. "Man is disarmed," Ellul says, "in the face of the perils threatening him, and is increasingly alarmed by these perils because he keeps reading about them."[16] Consciousness of all these dangers, coupled with

---

[13] *Existentialist Thinkers and Thought* (New York: The Citadel Press, 1966), p. 66.

[14] F. H. Heinemann, *Existentialism and the Modern Predicament* (New York: Harper Torchbooks, 1958), p. 36.

[15] *Ibid.*, p. 37.

[16] Ellul, p. 153.

the concept of self-estrangement, brings on this anxiety; the person becomes bewildered and frightened, and, as George Novack says, "such bewildered and frightened individuals can not help questioning their most trustworthy values and cherished creeds."[17]

For many people, anxiety is brought on—or heightened—by a sense of loss of personhood, a sense of insignificance in the face of increasing State and social control. Such State encroachment on the individual, of course, has not just begun, but it is gaining momentum. Here is Roderick Seidenberg, talking about the conflict in the modern world between the State and the individual:

> ... it is interesting to note, during the nineteenth century virtually every free and noble-spirited writer from Tolstoy to Thoreau, from Kropotkin to Emerson, rose in defense of the Great Tradition and the integrity of the individual against the steady encroachments of the state. But today it is no longer the state alone that is in conflict with the implications of these doctrines: it is a wider system of things wherein the state itself, in its supreme and sovereign aspects, is being drawn into the orbit of largr, worldwide agglomerations. Nor will the totalitarian pattern that has crept from the state fail to emerge in these larger spheres of international scope. ... As the gravitational force of the mass increases, that of the individual decreases, relatively as well as actually, until a final condition of solidarity and conformity is attained.[18]

Seidenberg sees in the future an "ultimate stabilization of human relationships" and an "abatement and exclusion of all change and variation"; thus, at length, predicts Seidenberg, man will find himself "in an ever more securely established milieu—in a period of unchanging continuity."[19] For some, these may be comforting words—but for the existentialist who prizes freedom, change, and the combative spirit, they are anything but comforting. But, while they are not comforting to the existentialist, they are not debilitating—in fact, they simply describe a state that must be faced and transcended.

---

[17] George Novack (ed.), *Existentialism versus Marxism* (New York: Dell Publishing Co.—Delta Books, 1966), p. 7.

[18] Roderick Seidenberg, *Posthistoric Man: An Inquiry* (New York: The Viking Press, 1974), pp. 230-31.

[19] *Ibid.*, p. 237.

Social and Journalistic Causes for Pessimism

The individual looks around him and sees a multitude of problems. He has good reason to be pessimistic. He has good reason to be anxious. He even has good reason to be forlorn and dismal in his outlook. Corruption is to be found on all sides; crime is increasing; population is getting out of hand; the world seems to be fast losing its capacity for hope; pornography is proliferating; brainpower is being mobilized for destructive purposes; personal safety is being increasingly endangered; millions are living a marginal existence on the brink of starvation; a sense of morality is almost totally absent in business and politics; educational standards are crumbling; illiteracy is growing—and there are innumerable other signs portending a dismal future.

The situation in journalism itself is equally dismal. Freedom in journalism is disappearing everywhere; a "sameness" is spreading throughout the press as journalistic monopolies and conglomerates increase; advertising is fast encasing journalism in a slick, emotional, irrational, and propagandistic patina, corrosive to cultured thought and language; journalism education— ever more "professional" in the sense of becoming standardized—is pouring out increasing numbers of poorly educated, mechanistic robots who find it difficult to write a correct sentence; and the public itself—and not only the government—is becoming suspicious of the press, finding it careless, inaccurate, unbelievable, and generally unreliable. Any person who has first-hand knowledge of an event and sees a report of it in the press knows very well how superficial, distorted, and inaccurate modern journalism is. Journalism is, indeed, increasingly under fire. And there are few indications that it is heading toward better days.

H. L. Mencken would have plenty of support today for his words about the press, written in 1920: "What ails the newspapers of the United States primarily . . . is the fact that their gigantic commercial development compels them to appeal to larger and larger masses of undifferentiated men, and that the truth is a commodity that the masses of undifferentiated men cannot be induced to buy."[20] And these biting words of Mencken still produce nods of approval today:

---

[20] H. L. Mencken, *A Gang of Pecksniffs*, ed. by Theo Lippman, Jr. (New Rochelle, N.Y.: Arlington House, 1975), p. 64.

The *average* American newspaper, *especially* of the so-called better sort, has the intelligence of a Baptist evangelist, the courage of a rat, the fairness of a Prohibitionist boob-bumper, the information of a high-school janitor, the taste of a designer of celluloid valentines, and the honor of a police-station lawyer.[21]

Mencken saw the newspapers (and they are still seen by many today) as being in the business of "snouting out and exhibiting new and startling horrors, atrocities, impending calamities, tyrannies, villainies, enormities, mortal perils, jeopardies, outrages, catastrophies—first snouting out and exhibiting them, and then magnificently circumventing and disposing of them."[22] Perhaps Mencken's harshest indictments of the American newspaper are found in this passage:

It is a mass of trivialities and puerilities; to recite it would be to make even a barber beg for mercy. What is missing from it, in brief, is everything worth knowing—everything that enters into the common knowledge of educated man. There are managing editors in the United States, and scores of them, who have never heard of Kant or Johannes Muller and never read the Constitution of the United States; there are city editors who do not know what a symphony is, or a streptococcus, or the Statute of Frauds; there are reporters by the thousands who could not pass the entrance examination for Harvard or Tuskegee, or even Yale. It is this vast and militant ignorance, this widespread and fathomless prejudice against intelligence, that makes American journalism so pathetically feeble and vulgar, and so generally disreputable.[23]

More recently (in 1971) Herbert I. Schiller has noted that "the information process in the United States continues to rest firmly in the grip of tenacious stand-patters." He further opines that these "stand-patters" are simply not capable of doing the job of explaining to their audiences the changes which are appearing in society—at home and abroad.[24] Schiller blasts the American press for being propagandistic, imperialistic, anti-progressive, etc., in this extremely critical appraisal of U.S. journalism.

Even Edward J. Epstein, a press critic whose comments on the press are generally considered moderate, has said that it is

---

[21] *Ibid.*, p. 63.

[22] *Ibid.*, p. 65.

[23] *Ibid.*, p. 130-131.

[24] Herbert I. Schiller, *Mass Communications and American Empire* (Boston: Beacon Press, 1971), p. 154.

practically impossible for Americans to get the truth from the press. He notes that Walter Lippmann also had concluded pessimistically "that if the public required a more truthful interpretation of the world they lived in, they would have to depend on institutions other than the press."[25] Epstein adds that journalists cannot claim authority (such as that granted to academic researchers) because they cannot fulfill the requirements of always identifying their sources, and he says that "without identifiable sources the account cannot be reviewed or corroborated by others with specialized knowledge of the subject," and that therefore "even the most egregious errors may thus remain uncorrected."[26]

Ben Bagdikian, another contemporary press critic, writing of the large American daily newspapers, says that "a few are excellent, more are mediocre, and many are wretched."[27] And, as to the small dailies and weeklies in America, Bagdikian believes they are "the backyard of the trade, repositories for any piece of journalistic junk tossed over the fence, run as often by the printshop proprietors as by editors."[28] And, Jack Anderson, a reporter who evidences many existentialist traits, raps the press for not doing enough investigative reporting and for being too timid and passive. "Investigative reporters," he says, "must work harder, dig deeper, and verify their facts more carefully than establishment reporters."[29]

I, myself, could add many other negative observations about the press which would bespeak of the pessimistic outlook which can be taken by the journalist (or any other person) as he looks about the journalistic landscape. However, I shall refrain from doing this at present, and simply say that the basic "corporate" nature of the mass media and the increasing conformity and depersonalization found in all parts of our journalism is what I see as the most pessimistic indicator for the future. And from this conformist tendency emerges the dismal conclusion (at least for all libertarians and existentialists): that press freedom generally,

---

[25] Edward J. Epstein, *Between Fact and Fiction: The Problem of Journalism* (New York: Random House—Vintage Books, 1975), p. 4.

[26] *Ibid.*, p. 8.

[27] Ben Bagdikian, *The Effete Conspiracy and Other Crimes by the Press* (New York: Harper & Row—Colophon Books, 1974), p. 8.

[28] *Ibid.*, p. 47.

[29] Jack Anderson, *The Anderson Papers* (New York: Random House—Ballantine Books, 1974), p. 9.

and personal journalistic autonomy specifically, is lying on the sickbed throughout the world at the very door of death.

The Specter of Technology and Organization

One of the chief dangers to press freedom (and to freedom generally) is the impact of technology and organization on the individual life of a person. The journalist finds that he has less and less incentive, encouragement, or chance to exert his own creativity; he knows that his organization demands more and more of his time and effort. He conforms or he suffers. So generally he conforms. What else can he do? This is the normal question which he asks; and this question presents his rationalization for submitting himself to the encroachment of technology and organization.

He can, of course, rebel. He can meet the life-facts and life-forces head-on. He can agitate. He can individualize himself through *his attitude* toward technology and organization. He can know that this attitude forces him to fight constantly to retain as much self-determinism and self-respect as possible. Certainly, he can not escape the benumbing influence of technology altogether; but he can fling himself enthusiastically into the fight for self-preservation. He can glory in the *tension* of the struggle. For he knows that when the struggle stops—and he capitulates to the machine and the organization—*as a person* he is dead.

And, of course, he can always change jobs. He can quit if the restrictions become so strict that he is unable even to struggle against them. But this is not the existential journalist's way: he prefers to remain in the fray—not in order to change the organization to *his* type of organization, for he is against *all* organizations. He wants to stay in the struggle for the simple reason that the intensity and constant tension is where real life is. In spite of this proclivity to struggle, the existential journalist recognizes the fact that growing technology and organization are forces which level society and make it more difficult for the person to direct his own life. In this sense he can look on organization (and its accompanying technology) as degrading to the person, as tragic barriers to self-fulfillment, and as potent contributors to a pessimistic outlook.

Organizations exert a great pull on the individual. In journalism this is especially true; for not only the complexity of the news institution itself, with its proliferating hierarchy, but the expanding reliance on computers and other machines that increasingly take decisions out of the hands of the individual journalist. Michael Novak bemoans this growing embrace of scientism in these words:

> The more science and technology advance, the clearer their inner dynamic becomes. They are not directed toward the good of concrete, individual human beings but toward efficiency. The primary goal of scientific knowledge is power; the primary goal of technology is efficiency. Neither power nor efficiency has a necessary relation to the integrity of persons.[30]

The journalist is easily caught up in the organization. He is, as H. L. Mencken has noted, "forced to make himself an instrument of enterprises that he sometimes cannot understand and must often regard as sinister." How does this affect him? Mencken adds that the journalist "ends by losing all sense of public responsibility, and so becomes a mere kept blackguard, ready at the word of command to defend the guilty or to harass and persecute the innocent."[31] The journalist is prone to become "an instrument," as Mencken calls him, because of the temptation to lose himself in the organization; in a real sense the average journalist wants to conform, to operate in highly predictable and harmonious ways. What Lewis Yablonsky calls "robopathic patterns" are insidious; they are prone to dominate rather quickly any newspaper or other journalistic medium. They creep in, spread, and subtly dehumanize the editorial staff until it becomes nothing more than a corporate mill, grinding out its routine and bland products in ever more impersonal ways.[32]

Unfortunately, it is very difficult (all but impossible) for the journalist to work independently; he is forced by the nature of

---

[30] Michael Novak, *The Experience of Nothingness* (New York: Harper Colophon Books, 1971), p. 34.

[31] Mencken, pp. 60-70.

[32] The routinized and highly structured world of pragmatic journalism affects the practitioner greatly, making him a good "organization" man, causing him to respect the hierarchy, to take orders docilely from his "superiors." The average journalist is shaped rather quickly into a good "team player," and this is why so often when these persons gravitate to the faculties of schools and departments of journalism, they have a difficult time understanding the academic life with its spirit of individualism. They miss the "order," the smooth-functioning of their old mass medium, and they are irritated and often stunned by the seeming chaos and independence of the "academic types."

journalism to be a part of an organization—to "join" a mass medium. This fact, at the outset, limits his individuality and diminishes his Self. And this very fact is what has caused some potentially good journalists, like Ernest Hemingway, to leave journalism for literature—or, at last to practice journalism only occasionally and peripherally.

In view of the basic nature of journalism, it is easy to see why the existentialist finds in journalism a difficult and unsympathetic home. He enters journalism normally by sublimating his individuality to the organization; he forfeits his creativity to the "system"; he permits the editors to change—and often mutilate—his copy; he passes his day writing what he is told to write, doing what he is told to do; he has little incentive or energy to "do his own thing."

If the average journalist stopped to think about it, he would realize that he, like Camus' Sisyphus, is constantly rolling the heavy stone of news and opinion up the hill of daily journalism only to have it slide back down the slippery slope; he goes on with this routine rolling throughout his journalistic life, repetitiously repeating his tasks—doing the same old journalistic tasks in the same old ways—day after day after day. Most journalists, however, *do not stop to think about it.* They are oblivious to this meaninglessness of their journalism. But the existential journalist does think about it, and this consciousness of the basic absurdity of it all is what gives his activity meaning. Michael Novak puts it this way:

> I perceive the ambiguity of my own conscious life. I recognize the formlessness, the aimlessness, and the disunity implicit in my own insignificance, my mortality, my ultimate dissolution. I peer into madness, chaos, and death. These insights are true insights. Not to experience them is to evade the character of one's own consciousness. It is to live a lie. The experience of nothingness bears the taste of honesty.[33]

In order to try to escape the aimlessness, the pain and anxiety of the existential situation, most journalists submit to the organization and lose themselves in the system. The organizing instinct is very powerful. Carl Jung notes the power of groupism and organization when he writes that "individual judgment grows increasingly uncertain of itself and . . . responsibility is collec-

---

[33] Novak, p. 15.

tivized as much as possible, i.e., is shuffled off by the individual and delegated to a corporate body."[34] Jung also notes that "people go on blithely organizing and believing in the sovereign remedy of mass action,"[35] but that "ultimately everything depends on the quality of the individual." H. L. Mencken blasts journalism for having too many practictioners who "are still slaves and they look and act the part," who belong to press clubs and who take a "childish pride in a puerile Philistinism, and are still far too willing to do anything they are ordered to do, absolutely without challenge."[36]

Fewer and fewer individuals appear capable of standing out from the conformist organizational types. Seidenberg, in his *Posthistoric Man*, writes:

> The dominance of the collective aspects of man is inherently assured; and with it the gradual conversion of the individual into a frictionless and depersonalized member of the community. For the individual as such will be absorbed in the shadow of his collectivized self.[37]

The conditions of modern life do, undoubtedly, arouse in the individual a sense of futility and personal insignificance. It is to this feeling of one's worthlessness that Kierkegaard attributes the urge to organize—to combine with others. Kierkegaard, one of the foremost opponents of this Hegelian emphasis on "objectivity," calls the "uncritical desire to join the group a form of mass hysteria, and traces it to a wish to be stimulated by others and to be drawn out of one's own emptiness into at least a quantitative fullness and stability."[38]

Charles Frankel adds his voice to those who believe that technology—in addition to organization—tends to enslave us. Technological innovations, he says, are often introduced "without established mechanisms for appraising or controlling or even cushioning their consequences." The engineers who introduce them, according to Frankel, make decisions which have enormous power to affect the quality and conditions of our lives; "if they came dressed as social planners many of us would regard

---

[34] Jung, *The Undiscovered Self*, p. 26.

[35] *Ibid.*, p. 68.

[36] Mencken, *A Gang of Pecksniffs*, p. 85.

[37] Seidenberg, pp. 112-13.

[38] James Collins, *The Mind of Kierkegaard* (Chicago: Henry Regnery Co.—Gateway Edition, 1967), p. 192.

them as tyrants," he adds.[39] Gabriel Marcel has been particularly critical of what he has called "technocracy"—the all-prevading power of technology and its nilhilistic misuse in society. Marcel fears that in a technocracy "men may become *submen*, more and more reduced to their own specialized function within the. . . machine."[40]

Never have so many seemingly "normal" persons in our society been so "sick," according to Aldous Huxley. These persons are "normal," says Huxley, "not in what may be called the absolute sense of the word; they are normal only in relation to a profoundly abnormal society." And, Huxley adds, their "perfect adjustment to that abnormal society is a measure of their mental sickness."[41] Quoting Erich Fromm, Huxley notes that these millions of "abnormally normal people" are well-adjusted, but if they were "fully human beings" they would not be adjusted. And, Huxley continues, the conformity in society is developing into something like uniformity—and "uniformity and freedom are incompatible."[42]

So, I think it logical to conclude from the swirl of quotations given above, that one theme emerges: organization and technology are making the majority of persons conformists, are depersonalizing them, and making them tame and timid "robopaths." The existentialist, of course, fights against this tendency. He would certainly agree with these words of Thoreau:

> Undoubtedly, all men are not equally fit subjects for civilization; and because the majority, like dogs and sheep, are tame by inherited disposition, this is no reason why the others should have their natures broken that they may be reduced to the same level.[43]

The Cyclic-Entropic Hypothesis

One of the main causes for pessimism among existential journalists is the belief that press freedom is dying throughout

[39] Charles Frankel, *The Case for Modern Man* (Boston: Beacon Press, 1971), p. 198.

[40] Heinemann, p. 153.

[41] Huxley, p. 21.

[42] *Ibid.*, pp. 21-22.

[43] From Thoreau's essay "Walking" in Carl Bode (ed.), *The Portable Thoreau* (New York: The Viking Press, 1947), p. 619.

the world. This is much like the basic existentialist awareness of individual death, and the *angst* or anxiety which the facing of this fact brings. In the context of journalism, the existentialist knows that he must face the "death of freedom"—and he is determined to make use of this freedom while it lasts. Or, at least, he is convinced that he must exercise to the maximum the freedom which remains; he is *existential*, rather than theoretical, in his relationship to freedom. In other words, he is different from many "libertarians" in that he *lives* his freedom, rather than simply theorizing about it, or urging it in philosophical discourse. The existentialist is *always* a libertarian, but the libertarian is not always an existentialist; for the libertarian may be a "theoretical" libertarian, but the existentialist *cannot* be a "theoretical" existentialist since his existentialism must be *lived*.

Many thinkers have contributed to the pessimism stemming from the belief that freedom is dying and that all of society—not just the press—is gravitating toward a time of authoritarianism, passivity, and conformity. Many versions, timetables, etc. have been proposed for this trend toward an authoritarian society, but in every one on the net result is the same: a nondynamic, passive, totalitarian society which discourages individualism and freedom and encourages stability, harmony, and Statist and organizational paternalism.

Karl Mannheim talks of an historical cycle reminiscent of Nietzsche and Comte; he distinguishes three stages of development—the medieval man in collective solidarity, the post-Renaissance man in individual competition, and the presently emerging man steeped in "group solidarity." It is this third category toward which we are presenting drifting—and it applies equally to man in Communist, Fascist, and liberal-capitalist cultures, for the factor which Mannheim sees as uniting them all "is the phenomenon of Great Society which the industrial revolution has brought into being."[44] The pull of organizations, discussed in the previous section, largely accounts for this drift toward conformity and authoritarianism, for, as Carl Jung says, "people go on blithely organizing and believing in the sovereign remedy of mass action, without the least consciousness of the fact that the most powerful organizations can be main-

---

[44] Brian V. Hill, *Education and the Endangered Individual* (New York: Dell Publishing Co., 1973), p. 111.

tained only by the greatest ruthlessness of their leaders and the cheapest of slogans."[45]

Roderick Seidenberg insists that the principle of organization leads to "the ultimate state of crystallization" in a society, which results in "patterns of frigid and unalterable perfection."[46] Man will accept this fate, according to Seidenberg, for he will feel that this "centripetal pull of organization as a kind of social gravitation, at once universal, inescapable, and beneficient." Seidenberg also believes that the principle of organization breeds more organization—the idea of "One World" illustrates this trend, says Seidenberg, and "it has been in process from the beginning."[47] Carl Jung notes that the individual becomes more and more a function of society; in reality, he says, the State "drifts into the situation of a primitive form of society, namely the communism of a primitive tribe where everybody is subject to the autocratic rule of a chief or an oligarchy."[48]

Seidenberg postulates that the present century is the Century of Transition: an interim period from historic age to posthistoric age, a final age of historic slowing down, conformity, loss of energy, smooth-running organization, and passivity.[49] He points out that there is no real reason to believe in limitless progress and development for a society:

> The readily accepted notion that history will inevitably follow a continuous course without break or climax, devoid of any possible comprehensive transformations, and basic and significant changes of phase, must be held to be as arbitrary, dogmatic, and essentially unimaginative as the contrary notion that history is a directionless chaos.[50]

This picture is, indeed, a gloomy one. Or at least it is a gloomy one to the existentialist who frets in social stagnation, however placid such a society might be. He hates to think of this future drift from "the organic to the inorganic, from the living to the mechanical," as Seidenberg has put it.[51] He, like Seidenberg,

---

[45] C. G. Jung, p. 68.

[46] Seidenberg, p. 180.

[47] *Ibid.*, p. 134.

[48] Jung, pp. 26-27.

[49] Seidenberg, p. 85. Cf., J. B. Bury, *The Idea of Progress* (New York: Macmillan, 1932).

[50] Seidenberg, p. 67.

[51] *Ibid.*

sees in this trend "the lineaments of a Spenglerian doom not only of our Western culture along with that of the world at large but, as we have seen, of the individual *per se* as well."[52]

* * *

This brings me back again to journalistic pessimism, a pessimism based on this drift toward authoritarianism and on the recognition that press freedom has a terminal illness. On the basis of this belief, reinforced by a whole array of writers (who may not have put it so bluntly), I would like to present a hypothesis which I am calling the Cyclic-Entropic Hypothesis of Journalistic Freedom and Development. Here it is:

> A media system or a single medium develops slowly in its initial stages during a rather static, non-energetic and conformist period, gathering momentum for a time during a more energetic and pluralistic period, and then flattening out into a more bland, less energetic, more conservative state where stability and lack of friction, coupled with a gravitational pull toward collectivistic conformity, sends the medium or system into an extended period of passivity or into the oblivion of death.

The concept of *entropy* is worked into this hypothesis for it is felt that it is quite consistent with a cyclic theory of social systems. Entropy is derived from the Second Law of Thermodynamics, which says in effect that all systems tend to run down, dissolve, lose energy. This tendency to "run down" (entropy) has been a theme applied not only by physicists and engineers, but also by social scientists and historians (e.g., Henry Adams) dating from the first part of this century.

Since journalism can be looked on as a system (also, its parts as systems), there seems no reason why the concept of entropy cannot be applied to it. So it is hypothesized here that media systems will lose energy, become passive, and conformist. Norbert Wiener, who has written much about entropy, notes this increasing conformity when he says that sooner or later there will be "nothing left but a drab uniformity out of which we can expect only minor and insignificant local fluctuations."[53] He talks about the whole universe dying "the heat death" where the world will

---

[52] *Ibid.*, p. 207.

[53] Norbert Wiener, *The Human Use of Human Beings: Cybernetics and Society* (New York: Avon Books—Discus Edition, 1967), p. 45.

be reduced to one vast temperature equilibrium, but the concept might also be applied to journalistic systems. Wiener presents, in the fact of this impending entropic disaster an extremely existentialist demeanor:

> In a very real sense we are shipwrecked passengers on a doomed planet. Yet even in a shipwreck, human decencies and human values do not necessarily vanish, and we must make the most of them. We shall go down, but let it be in a manner to which we may look forward as worthy of our dignity.[54]

Paraphrased for the journalistic context, this might be that journalists are employees of a doomed craft—at least so far as its vitality and freedom are concerned. Yet the dignity of the individual journalist and the basic value of freedom still exist, and we in journalism must make the most of them. The freedom-loving journalist will be defeated; he will meet frustration time and time again, but his struggle for freedom and authenticity should be such that it is worthy of his dignity.

There are many indications of the shrinking freedom of the press in the world; annual reports by the International Press Institute, the Inter American Press Association, the University of Missouri's Freedom of Information Center and other groups and organizations show a steady trend toward press control. This is all well summed up in John Tebbel's excellent little book, *Media in America* (1974), where a pessimistic picture is painted. Tebbel quotes Alexander Hamilton who said in 1788 that liberty of the press must altogether "depend on public opinion, and on the general spirit of the people and of the government." Tebbel offers this stark warning: "If the 'general spirit of the people and of the government' is the only guarantee of a free press today, its demise is assured unless that spirit changes in both the governed and their governors."[55] And Jerome Tuccille adds his words to the warning of Tebbel:

> If government continues its intrusion into the nation's broadcasting industry, it will unquestionably be only a matter of time before total control is attempted over the publishing business, the film industry, and virtually every other commercial channel of communications in the country. When this happens, when government has succeeded in destroying freedom of speech, free-

---

[54] *Ibid.*, p. 58.

[55] John Tebbel, *The Media in America* (New York: New American Library—Mentor Books, 1974), p. 431.

dom of expression—when it has, in effect, eliminated an effective *verbal opposition* to its own policies—we will then be witnessing the beginning of a genuine totalitarian regime and the final destruction of all pretense of liberty in the United States of America.[56]

Each existential journalist will, while recognizing the coming death of press freedom about which these writers warn, determine to slow its coming as much as possible through individual effort, to create what Wiener calls "islands of decreasing entropy." This, of course, will serve only to hold back the final demise of press freedom; it will grant more time, but there is no reason for the existential journalist to think he can reverse the trend. For the signs are clear all around us that there is a growing demand for "order" and "responsibility" in journalism, and entropy is associated with "order" and lack of friction—a kind of equilibrium and harmony resulting from passivity.[57]

This natural drift toward less friction, less energy, to a kind of running down of the human spirit has been seen as "inevitable" by many writers. Seidenberg, for example, calls this final passive stage of society or systems "post-historic"; it will be devoid of change, passive, conformist, endless routine—"not unlike that of the ants, the bees, and the termites."[58] This entropic tendency can be applied to social systems, and has been. In a volume by J. F. Klein (*The Physical Significance of Entropy*), a work based directly upon the interpretations of two outstanding authorities in the field of thermodynamics, Boltzmann and Planck, is found the following pertinent passage:

> The Second Law of Thermodynamics has no *independent* significance, for its roots go down deep into the Theory of Probability. It is therefore conceivable that it is applicable to some purely human and animate events as well as inanimate, natural events. . . .[59]

Freedom and individualism were enthroned in the Nineteenth Century in the journalism of the Western World. To

[56] Jerome Tucille, *Radical Libertarianism* (New York: Perennial Library, 1971), p. 107.

[57] Joseph Needham, *Time: The Refreshing River* (New York: Macmillan, 1943), p. 220.

[58] Seidenberg, p. 170.

[59] J. F. Klein, *The Physical Signifcance of Entropy* (New York: D. Van Nostrand Co., 1919), p. 90.

some degree, Western journalism is still so inclined; this has been the era of the individualist; it is, however, fast-disappearing and, as Seidenberg has said, "once past will never again return."[60] He sees the eclipse of the individual as implicit in all the trends pointing to the future. He states: "In the confusion of forces that confront us nothing is plainer than the steady drift toward ever wider and more inclusive social relationships and, by the same token, a corresponding pressure upon the individual toward great conformity, coherence, and compliance in ever wider arcs of life."[61]

In this final passive, conformist phase of entropy toward which we are headed, the creative individual will have all but disappeared; for when society "tends toward a condition of stability, security, and eventual sterility, the exceptional men are doomed *a fortiori* to impotence and extinction; for in that society either they will not arise or they will be suppressed."[62] Oswald Spengler sees this final entropic stage (his "Civilization" as contrasted to an earlier "Culture" stage) as a *scientific* stage characterized as "artificial, rootless," and mechanistic. It is obvious that the existentialist would find such a world not to his liking; for in Spengler's words this "scientific" world would be superficial, practical, and soulless, where life would be "no longer lived as something self-evident—hardly a matter of consciousness, let alone choice . . . but presented as the intellect sees it, judged by 'utilitarian' or 'rational' criteria. . . ."[63]

Toynbee sees this ultimate stage as an imitative, non-creative stage, also. The mass of people lack challenges and creative energy. Speaking of civilizations, Toynbee says that once a civilization has broken down, it follows an inexorable and melancholy path. He points out that civilizations (and systems, too?) grow best when conditions are difficult so as to stir up a high degree of energy and *elan* in the people. When challenge is gone, he says, civilizations begin to decay; conformity sets in, and energy dissipates (entropy accelerates). It is then that society enters Toynbee's "Time of Troubles," which would roughly correspond to Spengler's late autumn or early winter stage.[64]

---

[60] Seidenberg, p. 86.

[61] *Ibid.*

[62] *Ibid.*, p. 218.

[63] Oswald Spengler, *The Decline of the West* (New York: Alfred A. Knopf, Inc., 1926), pp. 352-53.

[64] Charles Frankel, *The Case for Modern Man* (Boston: Beacon Press, 1971), pp. 174-75.

Seidenberg sees this posthistoric period as a period of "stability and permanence" symmetrical with, if not precisely equivalent to, that of man's earliest period.[65] He views history, then, as marked off with a transitional period—"a period of ever-increasing change, tending toward a climax, after which man may again attain, in perhaps an equally long interval of time, a relatively fixed state of stability and permanence."[66] This evidences a kind of historical drift from instinct to intelligence, exhibiting determinism, and evidencing cyclic characteristics. And it leads from the creative transitional period (which is presently ending) toward a non-creative, uniform, collectivist stage. Man thinks more; at the same time society gets more complex; there is more need for social direction or social engineering to retain social equilibrium; populations increase; chances for mass destruction increase. Therefore, man will use his increased intelligence to plan for stability, to direct mankind toward a happy, paternalistic, stable world. Also operative here is the existentialist notion—described psychologically so well by Erich Fromm—that man's basic nature is "to escape from freedom," or to live "in bad faith," as Sartre would put it.

Nikolai Berdyaev, also, thinks a cyclic social theory is valid, and rejects the concept of natural continuous progress of social systems. He sees the present century as a transitory period between a dying Humanist phase and an emerging "New Middle Ages"—a disciplining phase, a time of social fusion.[67] In this new "disciplining" or conformist period into which we are heading, Albert Schweitzer sees a decrease in creative thinking and an increase in superficial "mob-mindedness" formed by various "manufacturers of public opinion."[68] As he described it in his *Philosophy of Civilization* (1949), the main problem confronting us is the ethical, and he agrees with Spengler that the verbal concern and emphasis on the ethical indicates the last gasp of a dying civilization.

Walter Schubart feels, also, that we are standing before a new period of social stability, ushered in largely by a pervasive fear. He sees Promethean (individualistic) Culture dying and being

---

[65] Seidenberg, p. 56.

[66] *Ibid.*

[67] Pitirim A. Sorokin, *Modern Historical and Social Philosophies* (New York: Dover Publications, Inc., 1963), p. 139.

[68] *Ibid.*, p. 179.

replaced by an Oriental (collectivistic-cooperative) Culture.[69] Schubart, like these others mentioned, rejects the linear interpretation of history with its continuous progress. He postulates three main developmental stages for society: (1) the Harmonious, where man lives consonant with the world, (2) the Heroic, where man has domination over the world, and (3) the Ascetic, where man runs away (escapes) from the world.[70] This Ascetic stage is roughly equivalent to Berdyaev's "New Middle Ages," to Spengler's "Winter," to Toynbee's "Time of Troubles," to Schubart's "Oriental Culture," and to Seidenberg's "Posthistoric" Period.

*   *   *

Now, after giving some background for cyclic theories and for social system *entropy*, I should return to the hypothesis presented earlier in this section. The tendency of press systems to "run down" and the growing inclination to conform and to come to a static, harmonious state (after going through an "energetic" period) can be blended into a cyclic-entropic model of development. This is what I have done in the framing of this hypothesis, especially relating it to the growth and later demise of freedom in a press system. And, I see no reason why even the individual journalist cannot be seen as going through the same progression—from childish reliance, to youthful optimism, experimentalism and energy, to mature intelligent and cautious action, to old age timidity, passivity, paternalism, and loss of energy. This, of course, draws heavily on Spengler's four-stage typology.[71]

In framing this Cyclic-Entropic Journalistic Developmental Hypothesis, I have drawn on many sources,[72] but have relied mainly on those indicated in the brief chart which follows:

AUTHOR(S)	CHANGE: ROUGH STAGES		
Pye-Lerner-Schramm	Traditional	Transitional	Modern
Merrill	Authoritarian	Libertarian	Authoritarian

---

[69] Walter Schubart, *Europa und die Seele des Ostens* (Lucerne, 1938), pp. 313-18.

[70] *Ibid.*, pp. 13-16.

[71] Sorokin, pp. 90-93.

[72] The main works of these authors can be found in the bibliography.

Seidenberg	Prehistoric Historic Posthistoric
Berdyaev	Primitive Humanist New Middle Ages
Schubart	Harmonious Heroic Ascetic/Oriental
Sorokin	Sensate Ideational Eclectic
Spengler	Spring Summer Autumn Winter
Huxley/Orwell	Tribalism Individualism Collectivism
Wiener/Klein	energy increase max. energy energy decrease
Ellul	"Naturalism" "Technique"
Mumford	Disorder Interaction Inflexibility

Drawing heavily on the implications of the rough models shown above, and considering as important many of the ideas expressed by various authors earlier in this section, I have designed what might be called a Cyclic-Entropic Developmental Model which, I think, can be applied to individual journalists, to individual media, and to media systems. If there is validity in this hypothesis (and I am *not trying to prove it* at present), it does suggest a very bleak and pessimistic future for the existential journalist. Perhaps it is even bleaker for the non-existential journalist for he will adjust to it without even realizing the corroding influence on his Self which it will bring. So, in view of the discussion which has just preceded, I shall present the following chart (on the next page) without further comment.

From Pessimism to Pragmatic Freedom

After reading the preceding sections with their themes of pessimism, anxiety, and the illness besetting free journalism, the reader may wonder how the journalist can continue to feel a challenge as he looks to the future. It is, admittedly, a chilling and dismal outlook, and the average (non-existential) journalist actually does not feel much challenge. He has settled into a comfortable, cooperative niche in order to avoid the frightening implications of the journalistic future just described. He thinks he will live peaceably and harmoniously with the institutions that increasingly subsume him, and in this way he can achieve the greatest happiness for himself.

The existential journalist, on the other hand, recognizing (and *persistently* recognizing) the constantly restricting freedom that surrounds him, takes this "dismal" future as a challenge, as the *normal* state, something to be lived in dynamically and actively;

CYCLIC-ENTROPIC MODEL OF JOURNALISM

Birth-Childh., "Springtime"	Youth "Summer"	Maturity "Autumn"	Old Age and Death "Winter"
Authorita-rianism → Authoritarianism	Authoritarianism → Libertarianism	Libertarianism Authoritarianism	Authoritarianism
Tribalism	Autocracy	Democracy	Statism
Groupism	Individualism	Collectivism
Tight Organization	Relaxed Organization	Tight Organization
Fatalism	experimentation	Optimism	complacency	Fatalism	passivity
Conformity	stability	Non-Conformity	unrest	Conformity	stability
Conservatism		Liberalism		Conservatism	stability
harmony		disharmony		harmony and stability
Growing Energy			Decreasing Energy

"primitive" "TRANSITIONAL" "Humanist" "Promethean-Faustian" "New Middle Ages" "Ascetic"
TRADITIONAL   "Historic"   EARLY MODERN   MODERN   LATE MODERN
"Prehistoric"   "posthistoric"

PERSONAL-ORAL MEDIA   PRINT-ELECTRONIC   ELECTRONIC-PRINT   AUTOMATION

Informal	Rather dull	More formal	Media, highly institutionalized
Interpersonal Communication	Institutionalized Media	Very formal structure
"Elite Media"	Mass Media & Specialized Media	Media as Control Agents
Simple - Scarce	Mixed - Bountiful	Simple - Mixed - Electronic
Cooperative	Adversary	Cooperative
Monolithic	Pluralistic	

he sees it as an invitation to combat, to fight against the encirclement of the system, to plunge into the tumultuous waters of journalism and flail out at the monstrous waves of conformism and depersonalization. The pessimistic future—or the existential journalist's consciousness of it—is what spurs him to persistent and courageous action. Gain as much freedom, be as original and creative, write as intensively and vigorously, as possible; relate to the journalistic problems courageously, and exercise the maximum autonomy or self-determination: this is the imperative of the existential journalist. Instead of retiring from the struggle because of the danger of it, or because of the meaninglessness of it all, or because of the gloomy future that lies ahead, the existential journalist takes all of this as an inspiration and a stimulus to live a more intensive life.

The existential journalist cares little about theoretical freedom. He is concerned about *living*—acting out—his freedom. He is dedicated to creating Norbert Wiener's "islands of decreasing entropy" where the authentic self can breathe freely as it pushes constantly into the future, gaining essence or substantial nature as it goes. He knows that to be a *true* journalist or a real person he must be an individualist—even a non-conformist.

Emerson's words pound instinctively in his ears: "Who would be a man, must be a nonconformist. He who would gather immortal palms must not be hindered by the name of goodness, but must explore if it be goodness. Nothing is at last sacred but the integrity of your own mind. Absolve you to yourself, and you shall have the suffrage of the world."[73] And here again, are words of Emerson which stir the existentialist spirit:

> Let us affront and reprimand the smooth mediocrity and squalid contentment of the times. . . . Man is timid and apologetic; he is no longer upright; he dares not say, "I think," "I am," but quotes some saint or sage. He is ashamed before the blade of grass or the blowing rose. . . . Insist on yourself; never imitate. . . . Every great man is unique. . . . Nothing can bring you peace but yourself. Nothing can bring you peace but the triumph of principles.[74]

Of course, the existential journalist knows that absolute and unconditional freedom is an abstraction; but he also knows, that

---

[73] From "Self Reliance," quoted in Raymond Van Over, *The Psychology of Freedom* (Greenwich, Conn.: Fawcett Premier Books, 1974), p. 112.

[74] *Ibid.*, pp. 118-36 *passim*.

within the wide limits granted to individual willing, he can make many decisions and exercise a tremendous amount of freedom. He knows that he must be free in order to be ethical, or to be "responsible." The existential journalist knows that he can always refuse to do something, to write some story, to interview some person, to change some headline. He can always say No, which for Sartre is the ultimate and final freedom that cannot be taken away.[75] But the temptation is ever before the journalist to evade such decisions and to "go along" with the system, taking orders and doing things which eh really does not want to do. As Karl Jaspers puts it:

> Man would like to be able to renounce himself, to plunge into his work as into the waters of oblivion, to be no longer free but merely "natural."[76]

But, according to Jaspers, the existential journalist can not so renounce himself and escape from his real being. Only can a journalist come to his own self, according to Jaspers, if he experiences "the harshness of the real" and plays an active part in the world—even though he aims at "an impossible, an unattainable goal." This, says Jaspers, is the "necessary pre-condition of one's own being."[77]

Nikolai Berdyaev writes of freedom as the autonomy of man, and as a love of truth, a concept which is compatible with the press libertarian (e.g., John Stuart Mill) belief that freedom of expression presents the best chance for truth to emerge. Berdyaev writes:

> Man is a slave because freedom is difficult, whereas slavery is easy. . . . The free man is simply the man who does not allow the alienation, the ejection into the external of his conscience and his judgment. He who permits this is a slave. The master also permits it, but he is only another form of slave. . . . It is the autonomy of man, as personality, that must be called freedom. . . . The free man is a self-governing being not a governed being. . . . Truth is always connected with freedom and bestowed upon freedom only. Slavery is always the denial of truth and the dread of truth.[78]

The journalist often responds to words of this nature with

[75] Barrett, *Irrational Man*, p. 241.
[76] Jaspers, *Man in the Modern Age*, p. 181.
[77] *Ibid.*, p. 197.
[78] Quoted in Van Over, pp. 227-28.

"How idealistic! How naive! How unreasonable! These people don't understand the realities of working for a newspaper!" It is a truism in journalism that one can't do his "own thing," that he must follow directions, conform to the editorial policy, etc. And this rationalization is always standing by, ready to be used by journalists as they live largely in Sartrean "bad faith" in their work. Sartre and other existentialists have been aware of the difficulty of being free. Each journalist, in spite of difficulties and dangers, has the freedom *to try* to accomplish his ends. As Sartre points out, "we cannot say that a prisoner is always free to go out of prison, which would be absurd . . . but that he is always free to try to escape."[79] And, as he says in another place, "the formula 'to be free' does not mean 'to obtain what one has wished' but rather 'by oneself to determine oneself to wish' (in the broad sense of choosing)."[80] And, if the journalist does not *will himself to be free* (even if he fails), he chooses the inauthentic life; for he must, as Carl Jaspers says, "on his initiative independently gain possession of the mechanism of his life, or else, himself degraded to become a machine, surrender to the apparatus."[81]

*   *   *

So, we see that the existential journalist prizes free acts. These, of course, have consequences, and the existential journalist must take these into consideration when making his decisions. For he is responsible for the consequences coming from his free acts, whether or not he anticipated them. He must stand behind his acts, his decisions, and must not give excuses or plead inability to go against orders. For he can always say *no* to orders. Peter Koestenbaum writes that responsibility for all of a person's action is uniquely his. The experience of responsibility, he says, is a constant reminder that his actions are his, that he is an individual, and that nothing can change that fact.[82] And, writing of consequences of actions, and a person's responsibility for them, he says:

---

[79] Quoted in Robert C. Solomon (ed.), *Phenomenology and Existentialism* (New York: Harper & Row, 1972), p. 462.

[80] *Ibid.*; Cf., J.-P. Sartre, *Being and Nothingness* (New York: Philosophical Library, Inc., 1956).

[81] Jaspers, *Man in the Modern Age*, p. 195.

[82] Peter Koestenbaum, *Philosophy: A General Introduction* (New York: American Book Co., 1968), p. 324.

My involvement with the consequences of my action is neither a
moral relation in the traditional sense, nor a sociological conven-
tion, nor a divine edict. That I am responsible for the consequences of my acts, because I initiated these and could have *
chosen otherwise—whether the consequences could have been
foreseen or not—is merely the recognition of a fundamental and
irrefutable *fact* of my nature and a *fact* about my experience of
being human, disclosed by introspective phenomenological
analysis.[83]

Many journalists fear freedom for the very reason that they
fear to assume responsibility for their decision. For when a
person assumes freedom he forces himself to throw off his
inertia, cut himself loose from tradition, and, what is most
important, he puts himself in a position of accepting moral
responsibility for his actions. There is a reluctance for journalists
to take this step toward freedom and responsibility. Here and
there, now and then, some journalists do arise to the defense of
freedom and speak out against the restrictions and limitations of
the prevailing system. But often their solution, it is interesting to
note, consists of an *organization* of journalists to do combat—a
"profession" or a union or a society—instead of assuming individually a dedication to personal choice and action.

The struggle for autonomy, freedom, and authenticity in
journalism is a personal struggle. In the face of a pessimistic
future for journalism where conformity and depersonalization is
growing and freedom is dying, the individual journalist must
wage continuous and personal war against the beguiling pressures to conform. The journalist—if he is an existentialist—must
be committed to protecting and expanding his individuality and to
taking action, in the face of personal risk, to frustrate the forces
which would enslave and depersonalize him.

[83] *Ibid.*

Individualism, Commitment, and Action

Human nature is not a machine to be built after a model, and set to do exactly the work prescribed for it, but a tree, which requires to grow and develop itself on all sides, according to the tendency of the inward forces which make it a living thing.

—JOHN STUART MILL, *On Liberty*

In every act of rebellion, the rebel simultaneously experiences a feeling of revulsion at the infringement of his rights and a complete and spontaneous loyalty to certain aspects of himself.

—ALBERT CAMUS, *The Rebel*

For, believe me, the secret of the greatest fruitfulness and the greatest enjoyment of existence is: to live *dangerously!* Build your cities under Vesuvius! Send your ships into uncharted seas! Live at war with your peers and yourselves!

—FRIEDRICH NIETZSCHE, *The Gay Science*

FAR TOO MANY JOURNALISTS cower in their corners of the newsroom, routinely making standard marks and pushing regular buttons, or trudge the noisy corridors of life like rusty robots set in perpetual and monotonous motion. They live only in the sense that they breathe, communicate only in the sense that they utter the expected platitudes, commit themselves only to their regularized duties, and act only in predictable and institutionalized ways designed to stabilize and harmonize.

These are harsh words. They are meant to be.

After more than a quarter of a century of dealing with journalists, journalism professors, and journalism students in most parts of the world, I am convinced that the great majority of them are devoid of a sense of self—of a sense of personal worth and unique potency; I am convinced that most go through their days contenting themselves with not rocking the boat, with not saying the "wrong" things, with not antagonizing those who might cause them harm or anxiety. Basically, most journalists are timid souls. They are devoid of individualism and authenticity and have found shelter in the safe coves of corporate journalism. They have rationalized their inauthentic existence by flying the insipid banners of group loyalty and institutional cooperation. "Harmony" is their theme song. "Cooperation" is their life's strategy. An unwillingness to individual commitment and a fear of putting themselves in positions of personal danger have led the typical modern journalists down the road to self-stagnation. Journalism today has, by and large, become a world of purring machines, operated by machine-like functionaries, harmoniously packaging standardized news and mass-approved opinion.

Individualism is disdained in the average news operation. The eccentric, the person with integrity, with a mind of his own, is being squeezed out of journalism. He is looked upon increasingly, by his superiors and his colleagues and co-workers, as a poor "team person," one who does not fit nicely into the corporate journalistic system. The journalist with his own ideas, his own sense of moral values, his own strict standards of language usage, his own journalistic philosophy—if you will—is looked on with suspicion, or even hostility.

This state of affairs has several causes. One, of course, is the natural inclination of human beings to "escape from freedom" and from the traumatic experiences which often come from exercising one's own choices and accepting responsibility for them. Another is the growing specialization in journalism which, naturally, decreases the individual's dependence on himself and pressures him to put increased faith in the total cooperative effort. And another cause, to be discussed further in the next chapter, is the system of education which tends to package neo-journalists in conventional ways so that they will be more acceptable in the status-quo, conservative world of American journalism. And, finally and perhaps most importantly, is the growing inclination of individual persons in journalism to give up their individuality of their own volition, to retreat into the corporate structure for financial and psychological reasons, and to conform to inauthentic practices which sap their being of individuality.

Individualism: In Pursuit of Self

The existential journalist rebels against the dismal picture painted above. He is determined that, in the midst of this situation where depersonalizing pressures are growing ever more powerful, he will retain a substantial amount of his individuality. And, it is this determination on the part of the existential journalist which assures him of success. He *wants* to keep his personhood; he is *committed* to keeping it; he *acts* in such ways as to keep it: therefore, he will keep it. Of course, it may be painful to him in many ways, but he has the sweet satisfaction of knowing that he has retained his integrity, his unique essence, his individual self.

Kierkegaard in his *The Present Age* criticized his society, and proved to be very prophetic; for this essay has been the source of much existentialist criticism of modern society; such recent books as David Riesman's *The Lonely Crowd* and William Whyte's *The Organization Man* are still repeating and documenting his insights.

The individual is dying, Kierkegaard pointed out; there is a drift toward mass society, and this means the death of the individual as life grows more and more collectivized and externalized. Increasingly, he says, the social thinking is being determined by what William Barrett has called the Law of Large Numbers.[1] Karl Jaspers relates this idea to journalism, noting that when the journalist performs his work day after day in a routine way, he sinks "into the fathomless abysses of oblivion."[2] And, of course, it is very easy for him to sink into such oblivion in the typical corporate journalistic medium. He works for a modern large corporation or organization, which as John Gardner notes, loves and promotes "stability," not efficiency.[3] With this natural tendency of journalistic media toward stability, a kind of mediocrity develops, and functionaries become ever more the "same" or equal. Mediocrity breeds mediocrity, Gardner has pointed out,

---

[1] *Irrational Man*, p. 173.

[2] *Man in the Modern Age*, p. 204.

[3] John W. Gardner, *Excellence* (New York: Harper & Row—Perennial Library, 1971), p. 31.

and organizations and labor unions protect their "least able members."[4] In fact, oftentimes it is quite obvious that organizations take a kind of pride in, and give various kinds of rewards to, their mediocre members rather than superior ones who pose some kind of threat (at least psychological) to all others concerned.

Any observant and thinking person, looking at the world of journalism, must be struck by the increasing conformity, the growing mechanization and regimentation, the submission of the individual journalist to an ever-growing number of authorities— in short, journalism is increasingly subsuming the individual. "He is drowned in the mass," says Jacques Ellul, "and becomes convinced that he is only a cipher and that he really cannot be considered otherwise in such a large number of individuals."[5] When one looks beneath the patina of "busyness" of the average newsroom, he is struck by the smileless faces, the over-serious demeanor of men and women going through unenthusiastic activities devoid of a spirit of vitality and creativity.

"The individual feels himself *diminished*," says Ellul. "For one thing, he gets the feeling that he is under constant supervision and can never exercise his independent initiative; for another, he thinks he is always being pushed down to a lower level."[6] And, Carl Jung notes that "individual judgment grows increasingly uncertain of itself. . . , responsibility is collectivized as much as possible, i.e., is shuffled off by the individual and delegated to a corporate body."[7] Very few journalists go against such regimentation, such collectivized conformity; very few of them heed Thoreau's words to let their lives "be a counter-friction to stop the machine."[8]

The pressure, the temptation, is strong for the individual journalist to follow a kind of "spirit of consensus," to give in to numbers. But the existential journalist strives constantly to follow Gabriel Marcel's admonition to reject "the fascination of numbers" so that he "can hope to remain at the spiritual level, that is, at the level of truth."[9] Nietzsche was certainly one who

---

[4] *Ibid.*, pp. 17-33 *passim.*

[5] *Propaganda* (New York: Vintage Books, 1973), p. 149.

[6] *Ibid.*

[7] *Undiscovered Self*, p. 26.

[8] From "Civil Disobedience" in Carl Bode (ed.) *The Portable Thoreau* (New York: Viking Press, 1947), p. 120.

[9] *Man Against Mass Society* (Chicago: Henry Regnery Co.—a Gateway Edition, 1969), p. 221.

recognized the accelerating trend toward the loss of the individual's importance; individualism was dying, he believed, and he felt that he should present the world with the heroic figure of his *Uebermensch*, his spiritual Superman. Like Nietzsche, Kierkegaard was troubled by the spread of "herd mentality." The two philosophers agree that the individual is being emptied of all value and engulfed in some organization, corporation, institution, or some dominant totality. Kierkegaard calls the typical person a "cipher-man" or a "fractional man," having his purpose and importance not in himself but only in a quantitative social whole.[10]

The existential journalist, the committed and active journalist, will daily seek his own individuality in the face of the obstacles noted above. He will strive for individual fulfillment in the very fact of fighting such obstacles, although he realizes that it is highly unlikely (or impossible) that individual fulfillment for many (on a large scale) will ever be achieved. For large-scale individual fulfillment would have to assume a radically different social system than is known at present. As John Gardner says:

> Individual fulfillment on a wide scale can occur only in a society which is designed to cherish the individual, which has the strength to protect him, and richness and diversity to stimulate and develop him, and the system of values within which he can find himself—and lose himself!—as a person.[11]

While achieving a wide-spread or universal journalistic capacity for self-fulfillment, there is, of course, the opportunity for existential minorities to individualize themselves. It is a matter of *willing*. It is a matter of the journalist desiring to be himself—or better, constantly and authentically *to create* himself. As Sartre points out: "You are nothing else than your life."[12] One of the chief reasons for a loss of personhood and individuality is a drift toward non-action, toward a kind of passive, non-involved state. Sartre says that the existentialist must involve himself and act on the old saw, "Nothing ventured, nothing gained."[13] When the journalist ventures, when he forces or wills himself to be himself, to take actions, he reestablishes and reinforces his own

---

[10] James Collins, *The Mind of Kierkegaard* (Chicago: Henry Regnery Co.—a Gateway Edition, 1967), p. 184.

[11] Gardner, p. 173.

[12] Jean-Paul Sartre, *Existentialism and Human Emotions* (New York: Philosophical Library—Wisdom Library, 1957), p. 33.

[13] *Ibid.*, p. 31.

individuality. When he stops, when he passively floats along, when he ceases *willing* and acting, his individuality slips away and he becomes inauthentic as a person.

Style: a Revelation of Self

The journalist who desires to be an individual, who wants to be as authentic as possible, will naturally push himself in that direction. He will endeavor to be himself as much as possible within the obvious limits which journalism as a social institution permits. One of the most obvious evidences of increasing individuality is the *style* of the journalist. When a journalist cherishes his uniqueness, he also cherishes, develops, and protects his journalistic style, most obvious in his writing and, in the case of broadcast journalism, his speaking and "microphone personality."

Style is personal. It is the highly individualized dimension in journalism. It is through style that one's personhood breaks through; it is a revelation of one's self. The tendency is, in the evolving journalistic corporate institution, to hide one's style, to cover it up, to submerge it under a blanket of anonymity and conformity. But style is important and the journalist who loses it—or never has the real opportunity to develop it—commits a kind of journalistic suicide. He can, by treasuring and refining his style, strengthen his personhood. For, in effect, he *is* his style. Therefore, a negation of style indicates a negation of self.

Just as the existential journalist wants to *live* authentically, he also wants to evidence this existential dimension in the style of his journalism. He pushes as far as he can with his individualized linguistic probes; he gets himself into his written and spoken messages to the fullest extent. He opposes as vigorously as possible the concept of journalistic "neutrality" and dispassionate communication.

As the existential journalist's horizons change and broaden, so will his writing style; as he changes and makes himself, he is also making his style. He takes chances and experiments in his total life-acts, thereby manifesting his total "style" or personality; in the same way he must evidence commitment in his communication style. Flexibility of style is an imperative for him. He changes; his style changes. He is his style—or, his style indicates his truest nature or essence.

To change, to improve his style, the journalist must, first of all, seriously desire to change it. By wanting to change it, he evidences a fundamental desire to change himself, to push toward the future, to create himself anew—in short, to live existentially. He must change many of his normal habits and thrust himself into new environments—physical and intellectual. He must read carefully and critically, noting stylistic techniques which he grafts creatively onto his own writing. He must become conscious of other (and fresh) points of view, not necessarily to embrace them, but to use them, to benefit from them, to adapt them, to use them as catalysts to his own thought and imagination.

It is at this point that the journalist begins to change his style of writing—as he changes his *attitude* toward life and toward communicating this through his language. He has new ideas and impressions to structure, or to integrate with his old ones. The past style flows into the present and into the future; he has developed a dynamic style that changes as he changes—and, possibly, as the situation changes. As the existential journalist renews himself, so is his journalistic style renewed.

He sees new vistas, he hears strange voices, he receives different sensations, he contemplates unfamiliar ideas. He tries new techniques, he experiments with new forms, he pushes his ideas into new regions of thought; in short, he begins a new psychological and linguistic life and feels fresh intellectual winds in his face. As his horizons change and broaden, he breaks out of his confining prison of provincial and trite patterns of thought and action; he steps into a new verbal world, which, in addition to making his life richer and more satisfying, offers the verbal freedom necessary for the development of an existential style proper to a freedom-loving, authentic personhood.

Style can be honest. Honesty is an important aspect of authenticity and individuality. If a journalist's style is to reflect the authenticity of the journalist, it *must* be honest—meaning that it must spring from an unpolluted and pure Self. Style is the dimension of journalism that gives it power, individuality, variety, and charm. In a sense it is verbal magic. If the person is authentic, he will reflect this in his style; this existential style will manifest itself in language that makes a word sparkling, a sentence unforgettable, a passage stimulating, an article impelling and meaningful.

F. L. Lucas, long-time Cambridge don and teacher of writing, has said that the writer must (1) respect truth and himself, and (2) respect his readers.[14] These two facets of respect, as Lucas sees them, evidence the writer's honesty and courtesy and are cornerstones of good style. The implications here are significant. The journalist, in order to have a good style, must present his true self, however unpleasant it might be. He must be honest with himself and with his reader; pretense will find him out. Or, at least, he will find his own dishonesty out—and it will dissolve his authenticity. Honest style is really difficult to achieve—as is, of course, basic honesty—for the temptation is great to be eccentric, to be inauthentically impressive or profound—or, even worse perhaps, to avoid portions of the truth which might pain the journalist or someone else.

Honest style is style that is consistent with the journalist's being. It is style that participates not in hypocrisy nor delusion, but furnishes an appropriate (reliable) dress for the existential self.

If the journalist is a cliché himself, he will have a style that is cliché-ridden. The existential journalist will rebel against clichés just as he rebels against any influence that tends to depersonalize him and take away the stamp of his special, individual self. When one uses clichés, he escapes from himself; he loses himself in the vague, generalized and fuzzy forests of linguistic universals. He hides his real self—his real style—in Everyman's language. This is not the way of the existential journalist. He follows Thoreau's advice to be "resolutely and faithfully" what he is and what he aspires to be.[15]

The existential journalist, first and foremost, wants what might be called an "open" style. Openness is very important in authentic communication. Jaspers has called this "open level" of communication *Daseinkommunikation*; only through this honest and forthright communication can one recognize *Existenz*. Jaspers says it "involves complete openness, unqualified renunciation of the uses of power and advantage, and concerns the other's self-realization as fully as one's own."[16] The journalist as communicator is never quite sure that what he is signifying in his messages is truly what he wishes to signify, or—as Sartre adds—

---

[14] *Holiday*, XXVII (March 1960), pp. 11ff.

[15] *Thoreau on Man and Nature*, a compilation of writings from Thoreau by A. D. Volkman (Mt. Vernon, N.Y.: The Peter Pauper Press, 1960), p. 13.

[16] Hanno Hardt, "The Dilemma of Mass Communications: An Existential Point of View," *Philosophy & Rhetoric*, Vol. 5, No. 3 (Pennsylvania State University), 179.

if he is "signifying anything."[17] In spite of this constant communication anxiety, the existential journalist must try, and keep
on trying. He must be "open" and honest. In order to develop an
authentic style, one which he hopes will deepen the communication, the journalist needs first to be himself, to owe his allegiance
to his personhood, to drop all pretense and affectation in his
language, to let his own character and personality show through
in his style. This is really quite simple, but it demands courage
and a sincere desire to escape from the incapsulating world of
conformist thought, action, and language that dominate in most
mass media. One must, of course, adapt one's style to the
particular situation and circumstance—letting one aspect of style
dominate here, another there—but the core, the foundation, of
one's style is manifest in all of the existential journalist's work.

The main key, I suppose, is that the journalist must develop a
greater respect for himself, have confidence in himself as a
person and a journalist, come to the recognition that he has ideas
and a manner of expression which are just as important and as
individualistic as those of any other person, free himself from the
temptation to cling too closely to the general way of doing
journalism, and experiment with new ideas and practices as often
as possible. The need is for the journalist to launch into his own
verbal universe! This is really a psychological problem, and only
when the journalist has wrestled with it, and conquered it, will
he become himself, and will be free to develop a truly individual
style.

Daring to "let oneself go" and to experiment, and to cast old
concepts in new ways: this is the most important consideration in
style. In 1971 I was asked to write a "journalist's creed." Actually
I am not overly impressed with creeds and codes of ethics, and
the like, thinking them generally useless and trite, but I accepted
the assignment, "let myself go," and came up with one which,
admittedly, has many weaknesses. But it does show that journalism creeds do not have to be all alike. My creed, presented
below, was beautifully set in type by Thomas Bell, a printer at
the University of Missouri School of Journalism; he liked the
message of the creed and wanted to make copies available. This
creed will, I think, say something about individualism, and about
style in itself. So, I present it here without comment:

---

[17] *Being and Nothingness* (New York: Philosophical Library, 1956), p. 373.

(A JOURNALIST'S CREED)
DEDICATION TO *Language*

I dedicate myself to words —
  words that spill like flimsy fish
  through the nets of understanding;
  I would become a net-repairer,
  or build new nets of tougher fiber;
  I would constrain the elusive words
  that flash shimmering before the eyes
  and flirt with the mind.
I turn away from weak, wet words
  that wash away at the edges,
  and flop their frigid forms in sad gesture.
  I seek the precise words, the firm words,
  words that pierce to the inner core
  of consciousness with meaning and knowledge.
  I relish those words that alternately growl and purr
  as they rush to do my bidding.
I dedicate myself to language —
  to language that fits the occasion,
  to words that roll to the cadence of the message
  and spark the flames of excitement.
I dedicate myself to verbal precision
  that cuts cleanly through the thickened thought
  and seeks the crystal core of credibility.
I eschew the charred word,
  the undernourished and overused word,
  the weary word
  that flays away at thoughtless minds
  and drones drearily in dark redundance.
I seek words that grab the truth
  and cast it courageously before the crowd,
  intent always on directness and light,
  avoiding the dank darkness of delusion.
In sum, I dedicate myself
  to harness and use that ponderous pounding
  of language that restlessly rolls across
  the barrier reefs of perception
  and persistently probes
  the shifting beaches of humanity.

— JOHN MERRILL
1971

*   *   *

The existential journalist will have a style which is part poetic and part scientific. Like the poet, he must have a "feeling" for language and a desire to make something vivid and meaningful with his language patterns. He must learn, like the poet, to make his sentences say just as much as possible, and he must describe people and objects in the light of his own feeling about them. As the poet, he must try to create something that goes beyond pure objective description; the writer must add the other dimension of *self*, which largely manifests itself in journalistic style. The existential journalist is, probably, more a poet than a scientist, but he has some concern for the scientific approach.

He, at least, has a strain of the scientific concern running through him, but this will be kept well under control and used only to enhance the personalistic dimension of his work. Like the scientist, he will keep an open mind—at least a flexible one which will admit new data, however disconcerting, through the doors of his mind. He must attempt always to be fair, to be thorough, to be sensitive to differences while recognizing the value of categories and generalizations. Like the scientist, the existential journalist is an adventurer, an explorer—filled with curiosity and a desire to capture as much of reality as possible for himself and his audiences. He must be curious about what is over that proverbial next hill; this curiosity projects him *personally* over the next hill. He is really not satisfied to *hear* about what is over there; he must go and see for himself. He tries to get as close to reality as possible; he is dissatisfied with second-hand accounts, with quoting others—this is for the non-existential journalists. The existential journalist is a reality-confronter; he is not a dispassionate stenographer of life. He is a plunger-in; he wants to go and see, not to sit and listen. He is a "news-getter," not a "news-reporter." Or at least he puts his main emphasis on the "getting," the "immersing" in reality—and "reporting" or communicating this reality in a meaningful way is a by-product.

This is quite a different journalistic orientation from the more common non-existential one. In it, *reporting* and all other kinds of "sending" of messages is what is important: in other words, the *communication* is the significant thing, with the emphasis on the message. With the existentialist, while the message is certainly important, the emphasis is upon the *journalist* and his true involvement with the reality of his story. Certainly, the process of communicating this involvement cannot be denied, but it is not the major concern of the existential journalist.

Involvement, commitment, plunging into the reality of the story give authenticity to the journalist's account—and by projection give it its *real* meaning. These are the qualities which humanize the story, give it a dimension of significance on a truly human level. Dispassionate and "objective" journalism is for someone else—not the existential journalist. Objective journalism—a kind of neutral orientation, sublimates the journalist's authentic self, and signifies the death of "style." Perhaps we should consider more closely this whole matter of subjectivity and objectivity in journalism.

Subjectivity: Its Place in Journalism

The existential journalist has a deep-rooted respect for subjectivity; this is natural, for he actually "thinks about" the nature of reality and the ways it can best be communicated. He knows that the normal sense of "objectivity" enthroned by most journalists is suspect; he instinctively—and intellectually—knows that objective journalism goes beyond what is usually considered "objective"—beyond the "accurate quotes," the "correct" spellings of names, the highly selective bits of information which purport to "tell the story." He *knows* that factually correct stories do not comprise objectivity. He is convinced that neutrality and dispassionate writing do not assure objectivity in a story. He is aware, of course, that he does not really know himself what objective journalism is, but he is sure that it has aspects and subtleties not present in the highly regarded journalistic concept of reportorial "neutrality."

He agrees with Michael Novak when he says that so-called "objective reporting" leads to misunderstandings in American journalism, and something is needed beyond "merely objective or neutral reporting."[18] Novak recommends what he calls a "largeness of mind and soul" for reporters; this, he emphasizes, is "quite different from pretended objectivity." He points out, too, that "there are no facts 'out there' apart from human

---

[18] Michael Novak, *The Experience of Nothingness* (New York: Harper Colophon Books, 1971), p. 39.

observers" and that these human observers (reporters) become "not more, but less astute when they try to be neutral."[19]

Novak insists that a more adequate sense of reality must be established which will take us beyond the old idea of reportorial neutrality and lack of passion. The first step in developing this more adequate sense of reality, he suggests, "is to recognize that objectivity is a psychological state,"[20] that it requires the cultivation of specific subjective states, the disciplining of attention and selected thought habits, the selection of one set of values in preference to others, and the shaping of perception and other mental operations. The journalist's sense of reality is gratified, says Novak, when he thinks of himself as being neutral or "objective," when he has what he considers the "hard facts," when "the figures" are all there in front of him. For instance, in Vietnam the journalists constantly provided us with *numbers*; they counted dead and wounded, missing in action, miles of road, telephones, airplanes, doctors, and on and on. But, asks Novak, did all this "objectivity" in the form of "hard facts"—numbers—assure the journalists (or their audiences) a good grasp of Vietnamese reality?

Existentialists such as Buber, Tillich, Sartre, and Heidegger have attacked the emptiness of empirical, pragmatic objectivity so beloved by American journalists. They have said that this sense of reality is too matter-of-fact, automatic, and functional— and that such a concept of objectivity causes a loss of admiration for the human person.[21] H. L. Mencken, a tough-minded American reporter, was in agreement with this basic philosophical perspective of Novak, but he couched his observations on objectivity in more straightforward journalistic language:

> Newspaper men like to think of news as something wholly objective, but it can be so only under exceptional circumstances. In its ordinary forms it is not merely a statement of overt facts; it is some concrete individual's opinion of the truth and significance of those facts. He may try in all honesty to keep his customary prejudices out of it, but nine times out of ten they creep in, nevertheless. . . . It is, in truth, this admixture of opinion which gives good reporting all its savor.[22]

---

[19] *Ibid.*
[20] *Ibid.*, p. 37.
[21] *Ibid.*, p. 36.
[22] Mencken, *A Gang of Pecksniffs*, pp. 182-83.

According to Mencken, the reader wants this admixture of the reporter's observations, interpretation, and opinion in order to receive a "clear and vivid picture." The reporter provides this, according to Mencken, by working his view into the story, and "by illuminating that report with whatever wisdom he may have at his command."[23] For, says Mencken, "he can see only through his own eyes, and can weigh conflicting evidence only in the balance of his own judgment."[24] This idea is presented by Novak as the good reporter's "walking around events," in such a way as to show us "more than one interpretation of them, using his own skills as an interpreter to portray deep and subtle nuances of various points of view."[25]

The term "subjectivity" is normally treated by American journalists as if it were anathema to good reporting. And, perhaps, the modern dignification of "science" is largely responsible for this idea—for science is "objective" and everything else is "subjective"; science gets at the truth, and everything else does not. Hwa Yol Jung, writing on existentialism and phenomenology, deals with this point:

> The affirmation of objectivism to the exclusion of subjectivism is misleading because it ignores the place of subjectivity in thought and observation. What is observable (a datum), for example, is always related to the awareness of an observer. A datum of observation is not yet a fact, and a fact is meaningful only in relation to the observer for whom it is a fact. Thus a fact is nothing but meaning given to a datum (or data) by the observer in the process of observation. Further, the truth of a fact or thought for one observer is sanctioned intersubjectively—that is, by a scientific or intellectual community. As consciousness is intentional, reflect thought, whether philosophical or scientific, is neither entirely subjective nor entirely objective.[26]

Very often has the journalist heard such words as these from an editor or colleague: "Is it correct? Did the source really say that? Is his name spelled correctly? Are you sure he lives at that address?" This sort of questioning in regard to a story might be considered a kind of journalistic substantiation of objectivity. Seldom are these types of questions asked: "In what context did

---

[23] *Ibid.*, p. 183.

[24] *Ibid.*

[25] Novak, *Experience of Nothingness*, p. 40.

[26] Hwa Yol Jung, (ed.), *Existential Phenomenology and Political Theory: A Reader* (Chicago: Henry Regnery Co., 1972), p. xxvi.

he say that? What *else* did he say? Was he smiling when he said that? Did he really mean this or was it an off-the-cuff remark or joke? Is what he said really true?" These are the questions which seek to get beneath the normal journalistic concept of objectivity; they are usually not asked because they are hard to answer—and they force the reporter into a completely different level of reporting. They force him to think, to judge, to form opinions, to interpret, to attempt to give a "total context" kind of report. And they force him to get himself into the story. He is accustomed to giving bits and pieces of the event, strung together in rather juvenile paragraphs of one-or-two-sentences. His main concern is usually with what is merely "correct" (and even this he cannot handle too well), not with what is contextually true. And there is a difference.

Karl Jaspers warns that we need to be dissatisfied with "what is merely correct," and points out that often the truth is obscured by "a variety of opinions which are hung on the skeleton of a supposedly rational pattern."[27] Truth, according to Jaspers, is "infinitely *more* than scientific correctness."[28] What the existential journalist will seek, I suppose, is what Jaspers calls an "Encompassing." He distinguishes this from the objective, the particular, the accurate, the purely factual. It is a *larger truth*, a greater "objectivity" which has real significance and meaning. It is close to what William Stephenson has called *factuality* reporting, in contrast to *fact* reporting—a kind of reporting which tries to get at the "essence" of an event.[29] The existential journalist will be dissatisfied with merely reporting the "facts," selected and presented out of context and in a meaningless, unsynthesized, superficial manner.

This *Encompassing* of Jaspers, this *factuality* of Stephenson is similar to the German *Faktizitat* (facticity); it goes beyond what is simply "observed," and has to do with the inward, existential awareness. In journalism it would include more than surface description; it would deal with motivations, psychological states, feelings, etc. that would escape most journalistic reports. This *facticity*, as applied to journalism, has to do with

27 "Existenzphilosophie" in Walter Kaufmann (ed.), *Existentialism from Dostoevsky to Sartre* (New York: New American Library—Meridian Books, 1975), p. 175.

28 *Ibid*.

29 John C. Merrill, *The Imperative of Freedom* (New York: Hastings House, 1974), p. 154.

basic, fundamental aspects of persons and situations which are usually not considered important enough, or interesting enough to report—or, with the part which is deemed beyond the understanding of the reporter.

The existential reporter, however, will try to get at these aspects of the story. *What* a person is differs from *who* he is (a surface journalistic fact); the *what* includes the why—and a concern with this aspect gets the journalist to another level of journalistic expression. Facticity reporting, then, for the existential journalist focuses on the "state of being there," a kind of total context presentation, in a certain situation; the reporter must try to see everything from the perspective of the situation. In reporting a speech, for example, the journalist must not simply quote the *words* of the speaker, provide an outward description of the speaker, give the identification of the speaker, but he must try to "get into" the speaker's mind, to present his motivations, his feelings, and he must try to go beyond the actual words to an interpretation of facial expressions, gestures, raised eyebrows, smiles, etc. Also he must not forget the environment of the speech, the conditions under which the person is speaking, the audience and its reactions. A speech story, in other words, is far more than a stenographic record of the words a speaker utters.

Although it is contrary to most American journalistic practice and to most teaching in journalism schools, the concept of good reporting must also stress the *feelings* of the reporter. Usually the reporter is admonished to keep himself—most certainly his "feelings"—out of his story, but sometimes these feelings of the reporter are very important. As John Macquarrie says, the feelings are not necessarily "antithetical to reason and thought"; in fact, he says, they are "a source of insights."[30] Through his feeling, his sensing, his premonitions, and hunches, the journalist has a "uniquely direct way of participating in the world"; his feelings or emotions are a kind of register of his "being-in-the-world."[31] Often, these "feelings" subjectivize a journalist's report even when he is unaware of it. They influence, for example, his selecting a "story" to report in the first place, and

---

[30] John Macquarrie, *Existentialism*, p. 119.

[31] Martin Heidegger speaks of *Gestimmtheit*—being "attuned" to the world; Paul Ricoeur uses a similar metaphor when he speaks of *tonalité*, as if one had to adjust to the "pitch" of the world. See Macquarrie, *Existentialism*, pp. 119-23 *passim*.

they cause him to choose various parts of it, and to organize and emphasize and "play" this selected information in certain ways. In the words of Karl Mannheim, the journalist "imposes a pattern on reality which reality itself does not have when we 'report' or describe it."[32] This is a pattern which Mannheim sees as "a projection of our own interests or assumptions and not of the facts themselves."[33]

Erich Fromm is insistent that "subjectivity" is important in reporting. *True* objectivity, as Fromm discusses it in *Man for Himself*, requires more than simply seeing an event or object dispassionately and neutrally; it requires the observer to become related in some way to that which is being reported. The nature of the object and the nature of the observer must be merged and considered equally important if we are to get at what constitutes true objectivity.[34] Fromm goes on to say that

> . . . objectivity is not, as it is often implied in a false idea of "scientific" objectivity, synonymous with detachment, with absence of interest and care. How can one penetrate the veiling surface of things to their causes and relationships if one does not have an interest that is vital and sufficiently impelling for so laborious a task?

Fromm stresses that objectivity does not mean detachment; rather he says, it has more to do with "respect." And he points out that the idea that lack of interest is a condition for recognizing the truth is fallacious. All productive thinking and observing and communicating are stimulated by the interest of the observer, according to Fromm. And it would seem that productive journalism, or journalism that reaches furthest toward *true* objectivity, would also be that which involves the interest of the reporter. It is impossible for the journalist to detach himself from his story if he is to give an honest and full ("encompassing") account. For as Fromm says, "To be able to listen to oneself is a prerequisite for the ability to listen to others; to be at home with oneself is the necessary condition for relating oneself to others."[35]

---

[32] Charles Frankel, *The Case for Modern Man*, pp. 134-35.

[33] Quotation from Frankel, p. 135. Cf. Karl Mannheim, *Ideology and Utopia* (New York: Harcourt, Brace & Co., 1936).

[34] *Man for Himself: An Inquiry into the Psychology of Ethics* (New York: Holt, Rinehart & Winston—Fawcett Premier Books, 1966), p. 111.

[35] *Ibid.*, p. 113. This idea is reinforced by Michael Novak in his *Belief and Unbelief: A Philosophy of Self-Knowledge* (New York: Mentor-Omega Books, 1965). Understanding, he points out, assumes intelligent subjectivity.

Now, someone may object, "But what about facts? Are not facts undistorted and objective reflections of reality?" Facts in themselves, as we have seen, have little correspondence to objectivity. Often they distort and mislead. A fact, says Fromm, presented "merely descriptively" may make the audience member more or less informed, and "it is well known that there is no more effective way of distortion than to offer nothing but a series of 'facts.' "[36] Pictures—in a sense visual "facts," too—can distort, whether they are "still" shots in the print media or filmed or live shots on television. Philip Wylie has expressed well, in spite of his cynical tone, this point:

> . . . it is claimed that TV has made a greater number of Americans better acquainted with more truth than they were in pre-TV days. Nothing could be less correct. More people doubtless have a slanted half-glimpse of more events, ideas, so-called scientific marvels, the faces and voices of prominent people and so on, than they had before. But fewer than ever have any background for appraising these unrelated, unevaluated, and random bits.[37]

The sanctification of "neutralist" objectivity, against which Wylie writes, has become well established in American journalism. Journalists by and large pay homage to this concept of objectivity, wherein "these unrelated, unevaluated, and random bits" of information comprise objective reporting if they are accurate and verifiable. Of course, many journalists will take issue with this whole line of argument, saying that *any* good reporter avoids presenting "unrelated, unevaluated, and random bits" of information. All I can say is that the journalistic media are filled with news stories which provide superficial bits and pieces of inadequate, meaningless, and useless information. If the reader, viewer, or listener doubts this, he is invited to expose himself in a "focused" way to the news media, especially in regard to a "story" with which he has first-hand knowledge.

Without a doubt the "neutralist perspective" of objectivity dominates today, although the "Fromm-perspective" mentioned above is embraced by existential journalists. This does not mean that existential journalists always *succeed* in their total context reporting, in their "encompassing" journalism; it is a difficult task, and the reporting often falls to the superficial "neutralist" level of shallowness, but at least the existential journalist *tries* for

[36] *The Revolution of Hope* (New York: Bantam Books, 1971), p. 56.

[37] Philip Wylie, *The Magic Animal* (New York: Simon & Schuster—Pocket Books, 1969), p. 205.

something better. He is not content with the one-dimensional "neutralist" concept; he attempts to bring a greater degree of sophistication and honesty into his journalism. He is often frustrated by tradition and by a natural conservatism of plodding and unimaginative editors, but he keeps on trying. And, trying, he inevitably meets with some success even in the most stagnant and reactionary environs.

Action: The Proof of Personhood

The striving of the existential journalist toward a more "encompassing" journalism—a more subjective journalism—is an indication of an action-oriented perspective. On the other hand, the dispassionate, the neutralist, the nonexistential journalist who dominates today's media takes very few actions. At least, he takes few actions of an authentic type; for mainly his activities are routine, expected, predictable, institutionalized ones for which he can take no special credit. He has inserted himself into the giant journalistic computor and has consented in his own mechanistic manipulation. He acts, but his acts are those of the robot who moves this way or that when the proper button is pushed.

Action, I am often told by journalism students and journalists, is dependent on freedom; therefore, if the person has little freedom, he cannot act authentically very often in his journalism. Frequently a student will tell me that he wishes he could do this-or-that on *The Columbia Missourian*.[38] "Have you tried?" I ask. The answer is usually that he has not. He has simply assumed he could not do it; he felt it useless to ask, or to try. In this way, many journalists enslave themselves by their own inaction, their timidity, and reluctance to try anything that departs from the norm. "Keep pushing," I tell the students. "You won't be able to do everything you want to do, but you'll manage to do a lot more than you think you can do." For it has been my observation that a sincere and persistent person can usually get his way—or at least "part" of his way. But most never try, or they give up too soon; and they thereby contribute to the solidification of institutionalized activities and conformity.

---

[38] The University of Missouri School of Journalism's regular, competitive daily newspaper, run as a laboratory paper under the direction of certain faculty members.

Often I have found that, if you believe in something and want to take some action which is in the "twilight zone" of policy, the best course is to go ahead and do it. Often bringing it out in discussion, talking about it, arguing about it, getting it bogged down in institutional red tape, is as good as killing it. So the existential journalist should go ahead and do it, if he thinks it is the proper action to take. Perhaps one time out of ten he will be thwarted in his desired action, or he will have to pay some penalty for having taken it, but in the other nine times he will have succeeded; he will have pushed back the fuzzy limits of restriction; he will have broken new ground; he will have expanded his own world of freedom and the freedom-worlds of others.

It is through these journalistic choices that the existential journalist grows, matures, creates himself, and projects himself into the future. He must choose not simply to desire to act; he must choose to act. His actions prove his personhood.

The very notion of man for the existentialist, according to Macquarrie, turns away from "all static ideas and sees him in action from the first."[39] The emphasis is on man as "an agent," one who insists on action—on doing, not just "being"—for only in action does "existence attain concreteness and fullness."[40] For the existentialist, action does, however, include more than overt activities; it includes both thought and passion. For as Macquarrie says, if thought, passion, and inward decision are lacking, nothing will be left worthy of the name of action. "Thus," Macquarrie adds, "in spite of the premium that the existentialist places upon action, existentialism is not the same as pragmatism."[41] So we can say that action includes more than empirically observable deeds; it includes the thought, the *willing*, the motivations, etc. upon which the observable deeds are based. It is, in a sense, an expression of the *whole* person, and as a person acts, he is "both projecting and realizing an image of personhood."[42]

The non-existential journalist acts, too, as was pointed out earlier, but his acts come from a surface-level of self which is hardly more than a conditioned reflex. These non-existential

---

[39] Macquarrie, *Existentialism*, p. 135.
[40] *Ibid.*, p. 136.
[41] *Ibid.*, p. 137.
[42] *Ibid.*

actions express more about the institution than they do about the person's authentic self. The existential journalist is not a random-actor; he *thinks* before he acts. This "he thinks" is important, for it indicates a motivation to action that transcends a kind of institutional determinism resulting in patterned activities. *He* thinks; *he* wills; *he* acts. His action, in other words, is not a social reflex; rather it is a self-determined action coming from his very being.

Existential action, then, is not random, it is not thoughtless, and it is not simply socially determined. For if it were, it would not be authentic action of the type which would make the person grow, create himself, become.

As Ortega puts it, our actions should not be "random fisticuffs with the things around us or with our fellow men"; for if they are nothing more than this, he says, they have no rationale, no foundation, no serious motivation. "Action," Ortega posits, "is to act upon the environment of material things and on other men in accordance with a plan preconceived in a previous period of meditation or thought."[43] So Ortega insists on thought preceding action; for, as he says, there is "no genuine action if there is no thought, and there is no authentic thought if it is not duly referred to action and made virile by its relation to action."[44] Therefore we can see that thought without action is dead, and action without thought is inauthentic—a kind of subhuman—action.

In conclusion, I should like to make it clear that when I speak of existential journalistic action, I am not referring to emotional and illogical escapades based on passion or instinct. I am talking about predetermined action which the journalist takes on his own, resulting from his own willing. And I am talking about action which the existential journalist thinks is sound and ethical—action which will help reveal his individuality, his personhood, and his concern for himself as a future person-to-be.

---

[43] José Ortega y Gasset, *Man and People* (New York: W. W. Norton & Co., 1963), p. 29.
[44] *Ibid.*

In Search of Authenticity

Our own age is essentially one of understanding, and on the average, perhaps, more knowledgeable than any former generation, but it is without passion. Everyone knows a great deal, we all know which way we ought to go and all the different ways we can go, but nobody is willing to move.

—SØREN KIERKEGAARD, *The Present Age*

Let us affront and reprimand the smooth and squalid contentment of the times. . . . a true man belongs to no other time or place, but is the centre of things. . . . I actually am, and do not need for my assurance or the assurance of my fellows any secondary testimony.

—RALPH WALDO EMERSON, *Self-Reliance*

The reality of the world cannot be avoided. Experience of the harshness of the real is the only way by which a man can come to his own self. To play an active part in the world, even though one aims at an impossible goal, is the necessary precondition of one's own being.

—KARL JASPERS, *Man in the Modern Age*

IN THE PRECEDING CHAPTERS a survey has been given of the main aspects of existentialism which apply to what I am calling "existential journalism." All of the characteristics which have been set forth as traits of the existential journalist help to define what may be called *authenticity* in journalism. The existential journalist is ever in the state of becoming authentic. He is, in other words, constantly making himself more honest, more individualistic, more involved and committed, more active, more responsible, and more ethical.

Authenticity: the Elusive Goal

Perhaps the most central quality of authenticity in journalism is a passionate state of mind. As Kierkegaard bemoans the passing of the "passionate age" and the coming of the "reflective age," so also does an existential journalist lament the lack of passion in journalism. To be passionate—to be involved, dedicated, committed to action—is to be truly human; for, as existentialists point out, being born does not assure us that we are human. "On the contrary," says F. H. Heinemann, "it lulls us into pretence."[1] Being human, he adds, is not a fact, but a task; for we are "in constant danger of becoming inhuman."

And, it is very easy to fall to (or never to leave) the level of the "inhuman," for people generally "are inclined to laziness" and they are "timorous," as Nietzsche puts it in his essay on "Schopenhauer as Educator."[2] Men, however, are not as timorous as they are lazy, adds Nietzsche, and "what they fear most is the troubles with which any unconditional honesty and nudity would burden them."[3] To be authentic, to be more than "a factory product," according to Nietzsche, a person "must merely cease being comfortable with himself [and] follow his conscience which shouts at him: 'Be yourself!' "[4]

Existentialism, as we have seen, is basically a philosophy of revolt against mass men, against all of those who have lost their authentic selfhood in modern technological and group-oriented society. All the notable existentialists who have been mentioned earlier—Jaspers, Marcel, Berdyaev, Buber, Ortega, Kierkegaard, Nietzsche, Camus, Sartre, and others—have expressed their deep concern about the inauthentic mode of human existence. To escape from this inauthentic existence a person must fight constantly for true existence; for a person, Ortega states, is not like a stone which "is given its existence." The Spanish philoso-

---

[1] *Existentialism and the Modern Predicament* (London: Adam and Charles Black, 1953), p. 39.

[2] Walter Kaufmann (ed.), *Existentialism from Dostoevsky to Sartre* (New York: New American Library—a Meridian Book, 1975), p. 123.

[3] *Ibid.*

[4] *Ibid.*

pher continues in his *Historia como sistema* (1941): "Man has to be himself in spite of unfavorable circumstances; that means he has to make his own existence at every single moment. He is given the abstract possibility of existing, but not the reality. This he has to conquer hour after hour. Man must earn his life, not only economically but metaphysically."[5] He must, as Nietzsche puts it in *Thus Spake Zarathustra*, "go into the open air, and away from all dusty rooms" in order to be authentic; he must cease being a spectator, "sitting in cool shade."[6]

A person must constantly pledge himself to the future; he must "engage himself," and as Kierkegaard has described it in *Either/Or*, he must make some kind of "leap" beyond the immediate situation so that he commits himself to circumstances which have not yet become clear. For the existentialist, traditional and routine ways of doing things are anathema since they are not on a truly human level; there is no engagement, no commitment, and no real choice. Therefore, on such an inauthentic level, the journalist would be merely acting as an automaton and not as a real, existing person. It is through this choosing, this commitment, this willed action—as we have seen—that a person develops character and an authentic self. He chooses, he acts, and he accepts responsibility. As Koestenbaum says, "existentialism holds man fully responsible for his actions and inactions; it does not displace blame onto upbringing, heredity, and environment."[7] So, not only the willing, the choosing, and the action contribute to the journalist's authenticity, but also the accepting of personal responsibility for the action.

There seem to be two main orientations among existentialists: (1) concern with changing *directly* the outer conditions of men's lives—a kind of "external" rebellion, exemplified by Sartre, and (2) concern with altering society *indirectly* through changes man can effect in himself, exemplified by Camus. Germaine Brée has called these existential emphases the "Promethean" (Sartre) and the "Orphic" (Camus).[8] The Prome-

[5] Quoted in *Ibid.*, pp. 153-54.

[6] Quoted in Brian V. Hill, *Education and the Endangered Individual: A Critique of Ten Modern Thinkers* (New York: Dell Publishing Co.—a Laurel Edition, 1973), p. 56.

[7] Peter Koestenbaum, *Philosophy: A General Introduction* (New York: American Book Co., 1968), p. 322.

[8] *Camus and Sartre* (New York: Dell Publishing Co.—Delta Books, 1972), pp. 240-45 *passim*.

thean tradition in journalism stresses defying the established powers frontally, directly; the Promethean journalist is, as Sartre has put it, the extrinsic rebel. The Orphic tradition, on the other hand, stresses a transformation from within; it is more internal, passive, and concerned more with the Self than social reform.[9] Prometheanism, in effect, seeks to change the outer conditions of men's lives, whereas Orphism seeks to alter society indirectly through changes a person can bring about in himself.[10]

Brée, in *Camus and Sartre*, says that Sartre set two main goals for the journalist and writer: (1) to unveil, disclose to his readers the developing patterns of the social world, and to disclose and judge social weaknesses, and (2) to join action personally to thought, to close the gap between knowledge and practice.[11] For Camus, the task of a journalist is mainly concerned "with the present, with the practical needs of the moment" for, according to Brée, he was "not trying either to detect or to regulate the current of history." Camus's confrontations are mainly with himself; he may have to struggle against others, but he does not "judge" them.[12] In the opinion of Camus, each man is his own Sisyphus; this contrasts with Sartre's sense that his task is "the role of guide and teacher"—to force people to see their lives in clear intellectual perspective.[13]

Even though each existential journalist may be inclined toward Prometheanism or toward Orphism, if he is a true existentialist he will be concerned with both orientations. He will want to improve his society (fighting against inauthentic elements outside himself) and he will also be committed to improving himself (struggling against inauthentic inclinations within himself).

Authenticity in Journalism Education

Journalism educators have an important role to play in respect to the development of authenticity and to existential journalism generally. They can help to provide an environment where existentialism thrives, or they can create an atmosphere

---

[9] *Ibid.*, pp. 252-53.
[10] *Ibid.*, p. 253.
[11] *Ibid.*, p. 241.
[12] *Ibid.*, p. 240.
[13] *Ibid.*

destructive to such an environment. Usually, I believe, they participate in the latter enterprise, and there are several reasons for their non-existential stance.

First off, they themselves are "corporate" people, institutionalized functionaries, and escapists from freedom. They have come from newsrooms where they have been efficiently depersonalized, or they have spent most of their working lives in Academe where, in spite of many myths about academic freedom and the healthy toleration of eccentric and deviant viewpoints, hierarchical pressures and political game-playing have gone far in depersonalizing and frightening the professor. In either case, the average journalism professor is an "expediency expert," shedding his integrity and basic honesty for an assurance of flexible working hours, frequent vacations, regular promotions, tenure, and salary increases that are not related to what he actually does.[14] Both campus and newsroom very effectively serve as breeding spots for non-existential journalists.

In the newsroom, for example, each staff member finds himself in a well-defined little niche, having little freedom to use his individuality and creativity except in highly proscribed ways in very narrow confines. He may often think of himself as having considerable freedom, but really he has become ever more institutionalized and imbued with the "corporate mentality." Deep down, perhaps, he really knows that he has little real freedom—that he suffers far more from "manipulation" and "direction" from his superiors than his medium suffers from Government or other "outside" entities. He has come to think of journalistic freedom as meaning only freedom of the press (as an institution) from outside forces; he seldom permits himself to think about journalistic freedom *as it relates to him as he works within journalism itself.*

But, after all, this is the system. And after all, journalism *is* private enterprise; the media (at least the print media) are owned by individuals and are in the private sector. So it is only natural that the "boss" is in charge of his employees, that the publishers and editors, directors and managers, exercise control over their

---

[14] Certainly there are some notable exceptions to this general timidity among journalism professors. Some of the most intellectually active and courageous teachers I have known have been in journalism. Every journalism student could, I'm sure, name at least one such journalism teacher. These exceptional teachers, however, are certainly a small minority, not only in journalism departments, but anywhere on the campus today.

enterprises. Therefore, the force of capitalistic theory combined with the traditional employer-employee relationship tends to ingrain deeply (and early) a sense of individual impotence in journalists; by and large they are educated to accept a kind of subservience and timidity, a kind of corporation-mentality which permits them to step into the world of journalism with a feeling of security and stability. They are educated to be harmonious zombies, and generally, that is exactly what they are.

Journalism education must bear a large part of the responsibility for this state of affairs. For journalism education, however hard it may try to avoid it, is a force projecting students toward a kind of "vocationalism," replete with conservative tendencies. The emphasis is on functionalism, on technique, on conformity to basic objectives. As Fred Hechinger says in a provocative article in *Saturday Review*, this "new vocationalism" sweeping American campuses emphasizes careerism, with a natural tendency to screen out students who do not seem to fit some standard prescribed by a vocational elite. It is marked, says Hechinger, by conservatives (e.g., Gerald Ford's "new realism") and by a drift toward specialization.[15]

A kind of "indoctrination" has replaced "liberal education" as a goal in most journalism schools and departments. Concern with the "right ways to do things" is replacing a lively regard for experimentation, free-ranging intellectual curiosity, and a concern for and questioning of, established doctrine. Learn the doctrine and accept it; don't challenge it: this is the core of modern journalism educational theory. Increasingly, technique consumes the academic life of journalism students; it is true that this concern with technique is taking computerized and other technological directions, but it is still *technical* in nature.

More and more journalism programs in colleges and universities are increasing their "core" courses, leaving fewer and fewer "electives" for the students. At the same time journalism programs are eliminating basic course requirements in psychology, sociology, and philosophy, which once played a large part in journalism education. Foreign languages are going by the board—and this at a time when educators pay lip service to cosmopolitanism in all its aspects. English courses, once strong in the university education of a person going into journalism,

---

[15] Fred M. Hechinger, "Murder in Academe: The Demise of Education," *Saturday Review* (March 20, 1976), pp. 11-18.

play little part today in the journalism student's curriculum. But, the journalism student gets hundreds of hours of training in writing leads, headlines, advertising copy, reading news before a camera, and on and on. Strangely, however, he gets little or no theory and practice in interviewing—probably the most important "technique" which a journalist can have. This is perhaps because interviewing, unlike writing headlines or pasting up a newspaper page, is a "humanistic," rather than a routine technique.

To give maximum opportunity for the development of existential journalism, journalism education programs would have to change drastically; at present they are drifting toward more and more "professionalism"—toward more concern with mechanisms, methods, forms, and techniques. They are attempting to standardize journalism more and more, not to diversify it. They are concerned with giving students the "right" and "pragmatic" (traditional) methods so they can step easily into the "professional" world of journalism. Conformity has set in—even in so-called research courses, which often push a certain methodology to the virtual exclusion of others. Courses teach how to do this or that, how to conform to prevailing practices. Seldom are these practices challenged or questioned; seldom are experiments undertaken to see if new ways will work better or just as well.[16] What is emphasized is *not* the creativity of the student. This is too often stifled. Even when certain professors do permit some creativity, it must be well within the accepted limits of safe and acceptable deviation.

In my more than a quarter century of teaching journalism, I have seen the spark of creativity killed many times. Bright, ambitious, eager, excited, expectant students have come into journalism programs only to be discouraged again and again. They have largely been molded into uncritical conformists, beaten into shape by machine-like curricula and machine-like teachers, and by strict requirements of a lock-step program which gives each student a minimum chance for individual development. Certainly, the program which would best create existential

[16] When a journalism program does try to experiment and change traditional educational practices, as the University of Iowa School of Journalism did a few years back under the leadership of the late Dr. Malcolm MacLean, "professional journalists" and accrediting groups for journalism education manage to put enough pressure on the experimenters so that they are soon back in the traditional mold.

journalists would be as open and flexible as possible, offering the student the greatest chance to pursue his own special interests, to go in his own direction, with the least possible stereotyping. This is not the same as endorsing "permissiveness" (which signifies a non-concern for the student's future), and it is not a denial that the student cannot learn from teachers or that he knows best in all cases what he needs.

Perhaps one reason journalism students are not often intellectually stimulated is that their professors themselves are not intellectually oriented. Very often journalism teachers are shallow and superficial; often, too, they are dull and unenthusiastic. Of course, this can be said of teachers in any academic field, but myriads of students can attest to the general intellectual slovenliness and the lack of a catalytic quality in journalism faculty members. Unfortunately, too many of them are in need of an education themselves. Great numbers of them are jaded practitioners who have "retired" to Academe (and the number is growing rapidly); they run out of personal anecdotes very soon and have to think up "busy work" to pass the hours in the classroom, turning over more and more duties to student assistants. They seldom read; they are seldom seen in the university libraries; they seldom think and discuss issues and problems in journalism with colleagues—especially those in other departments. They retire into their own little worlds, reveling in the memory of the "good old days" when they were out there practicing journalism. They have very few new ideas because they don't think about vital problems very often. They don't dare encourage students to experiment and think creatively. Why? Because they don't do it themselves; it is small wonder that "lock-step" teaching is the rule, rather than the exception, in journalism schools and departments.

The concept of authenticity relates to journalism teachers as well as to practicing journalists. And one of the principal aspects of authenticity is integrity—a kind of basic honesty which manifests itself in the person's being himself, saying what he thinks, acting only in such ways that are consistent with his own ethical standards. Erich Fromm, who has been quoted often in these pages, has said that respect for one's own integrity and uniqueness is inseparable from respect for and understanding of other individuals.[17]

---

[17] *Man for Himself*, pp. 133-34.

When the journalism educator has respect for himself, he will teach existentially and will generally expand the existential horizons of his school or department. He will enthrone not only his own individuality, but the individuality of his students. He will insist on personalism, not impersonalism; he will encourage diversity in his students, not conformity; he will try to give free reign to creativity, not imitation. He will constantly attempt to get the students into "deep waters," encourage them to take chances, make choices, accept responsibilities. The existential teacher abides by Kierkegaard's advice to call to those younger than himself to jump into the waves—to "leap cheerfully, even if it means a lighthearted leap, so long as it is decisive."[18] Far too many who are swimming today, as Kierkegaard notes, are doing it in shallow waters. What the existential journalism teacher will try to do is to get the student out of these "shallow waters" of mechanistic thinking and acting into the deeper waters of intellectual concern where giant waves buffet them around.

What the existential journalism professor says is that the very base of journalism education should be intellectual liberation. Where this assumption does not exist, where education is understood in purely technical or professional terms, it would be better to eliminate journalism from the curriculum. What Peter Berger says so well of sociology can also be said of journalism as an academic course of study: "Sociology is justified by the belief that it is better to be conscious than unconscious and that consciousness is a condition of freedom. To attain a greater measure of awareness, and with it of freedom, entails a certain amount of suffering and even risk. An educational process that would avoid this becomes simple technical training and ceases to have any relationship to the civilizing of the mind."[19] If we in journalism education do not heed Berger's words and stress liberal education, creative thought and action, and intellectual freedom, we will join forces with other social pressures depersonalizing education and indoctrinating for conformity.

The concept of "professionalism" is very popular today in journalism education. On all sides I hear references to "professional schools of journalism." I hear talk of the student becoming

---

[18] Søren Kierkegaard, *The Present Age* (New York: Harper Torchbooks, 1962), pp. 26-37 *passim*.

[19] Peter L. Berger, *Invitation to Sociology: A Humanistic Perspective* (Garden City, N.Y.: Doubleday Anchor Books, 1963), p. 175.

a "professional." I hear about "professionalism" in journalism constantly, but I seldom hear a meaning given to it. One thing is certain: use of the term indicates a kind of growing elitism, a kind of exclusiveness, a kind of "special" in-group thinking which is growing in journalism education and in journalism itself. Specialization is probably at the root of this trend; as Edward Barrett says, "Specialization is the price we pay for the advancement of knowledge." He adds that it is "a price" because the "path of specialization leads away from the ordinary and concrete acts of understanding in terms of which man actually lives his day-to-day life."[20]

As journalism becomes more and more specialized, it is perhaps only natural that it would seek a "professional status" like medicine and law. There seems to be a natural desire to be "exclusive," to be prestigious, and the term "professional" seems to connote something with these "elitist" overtones. When someone says to me: "We have a professional school of journalism," I immediately wonder which schools of journalism are *not* professional. If they are all professional, then, of course, there would be no need to call any of them professional. So far as I know, they all attempt to accomplish the same goal—basically to prepare students to practice journalism. So, perhaps they are all professional, although I base my hope for the future of dynamic and existential journalism on the belief that at least some of them will be *non*-professional.

For it is my contention that journalism (in spite of pronouncements and ethical codes of "professional" societies like Sigma Delta Chi) is not a profession at all and that it should not be one. No existential journalist would want to be a part of a "profession." This would tend to suppress his authentic self, to bind him with rules and procedures, to insist that he meet minimal "entrance" requirements, that he be licensed, that he be given a code to follow or a creed to swear allegiance to—all of which would depersonalize him, make him a conformist, and give him little play to his will. The existentialist wants no part of it. He wants no part of a "profession" where some elite will be saying what journalists should or should not do, what their duties and responsibilities should be, etc. In fact, such professionalization would take away the pluralism and freedom such as still

---

[20] William Barrett, *Irrational Man*, p.7.

exist in America. The existential journalist sees this, and rebels against it. He wants as few strictures on his freedom as possible. He sees himself as his *own* profession, and he is committed to his own "professional" standards—and to no one else's.

The existential journalist considers consequences for printing this or that. He must make decisions as to what, how much of, and in what way, to print. In making these decisions, he makes himself as a journalist. He thrusts himself into the world, and lives harmoniously with his subjectivity. Many standard or Establishment *status-quo* (non-existential) journalists say that professionalism demands this or that. Why? Whose professionalism? Where does such a definition of professionalism—or of journalism in a free society, for that matter—come from? The only real duty of an existential journalist is to be free, and to take upon himself the responsibility for his freedom. And it is really to himself that he has this responsibility—to his existential self, to his values, insights, beliefs, commitments. It is thus that he becomes truly authentic, a *real* journalist, not a puppet-journalist, one moving to the cadence of the group or the dictates of the editor or publisher.

Making as many personal decisions as possible, the existential journalist exercises his freedom; he exercises his editorial prerogative to the maximum, just as the editor does. In fact, the existential reporter *is* an editor. He determines what will be news and what kind of news it will be; he fashions it, makes it, subjugates it to his will. He makes the world in his own image—and, in reality, makes the world for his audience. He subjectivizes constantly, and cannot escape it; his newsstories cannot transcend himself; they are subjective simply because he is the reporting *subject*. He must recognize this, assert it, confirm it—and certainly he should not apologize for it. Why should he try to blot himself out by affirming neutralism and "objectivity"?

Standard journalism deemphasizes the journalist and emphasizes the reportorial object or the "issue" under discussion. Existential journalism emphasizes the journalist; it is *through* him, not *by* him, that we get a glimpse of the world beyond our direct and immediate perception. The existential journalist's perceptions, sensitivities, judgments, evaluations, and the like, *are part of* the reality of the situation and should not be sublimated in the name of objectivity. Standard journalism distorts through stressing objectivity—which is really a sort of pseudo-journalism, depersonalized and mechanistic to the point of confusing fact with reality, accuracy with truth. The existential journalist knows better; he knows he is a *subject* and not an object, and that he as a reporter must, therefore, be subjective. Subjectivity is valued and used, not apologized for.

Returning to journalism education, it should be noted that very little of the existential perspectives noted above have deep roots (or any roots at all) in the Journalistic Mills of Academe. Very few professors are existentialists. Fewer administrators are existentialists. And, for many, many persons—probably for the vast majority of those who read these words—this is a fortunate situation; for an existentialist emphasis is likely seen as a great danger to smooth-running academic productivity. Would not existentialism, many ask, make inoperative a sound philosophy of education—which, by its very nature, implies considerable conformity and indoctrination?

But, actually, there is no real need for academic administrators or their bosses on boards and in legislatures to worry too much about the rise of journalistic existentialism. And there is no need for the publishers of newspapers and magazines, the directors of broadcasting stations, to become anxious about their loss of power in the face of an existential revolution in their media: for the existential journalist is not good at organizing—in fact, he rebels against it—and the individualistic existentialist is hardly to be considered a potent force against the giant institutionalized power bureaucracy of the American mass media or the American university. The existential journalist and journalism educator will fight; they will struggle; they will do their bit against the "system" here and there, but they will not make substantial changes in the ever-enlarging conformity which is encircling us all.

Ethics and Authenticity

It is difficult to discuss ethics from the existential perspective. This is because of the very personal, *self*-deterministic nature of existentialism. And generally the subject of ethics carries with it a *social*-deterministic emphasis. We often assume that an ethics is formulated and enforced by some group of peers or by society at large. For example, we speak of legal ethics, or medical ethics, or social ethics. And, therefore, it is natural that those in journalism think about "journalistic ethics," implying some normative rules or standards to which *those in journalism* are somehow bound. This is a concept of ethics which, in a sense, binds the journalist to the norms of *the group*, leads him into a kind of conformist posture. And, what is more, in most cases the journalist has little or nothing to do with the formulation of the ethical code that bears on him. Little wonder the existential journalist has little faith in, or obligation to, codes of ethics.

Let us look briefly at one such journalistic code. In 1973 the Society of Professional Journalists, Sigma Delta Chi, adopted a "Code of Ethics." It, like most ethical codes, is an organizational code, filled with generalizations and semantically foggy clichés. Such phrases stating that SDX'ers believe in "public enlightenment as the forerunner of justice," "obligations that require journalists to perform with intelligence, objectivity, accuracy, and fairness," and serving "the general welfare" are to be found.

The Code enthrones "responsibility" and declares that journalists "who use their professional status as representatives of the public for selfish or other unworthy motives violate a high trust." Existential journalists will be surprised to hear that SDX considers them as having "professional status" or that selfish motives are naturally "unworthy." Then, the Code proceeds to state such vague glittering generalities as that "journalists uphold the right to speak unpopular opinions and the privilege to agree with the majority." One interesting statement in the Code is that journalists "must be free of obligation to any interest other than the public's right to know the truth." If that is really the case, then why does SDX come out with a Code of Ethics, in which it attempts to place many *other* obligations on the journalists?

The SDX Code runs through the usual litany of "don'ts"—such as not taking gifts, free trips, special treatment, and secondary employment. We are even told that journalists should refrain from "political involvement, holding office, and service in community organizations"; such activities are all right, of course, if they do not compromise "the integrity of journalists and their employers." Then, the Code tells SDX members that "so-called news communications from private sources should not be published or broadcast without substantiation of their claims to news value." This is indeed a strange statement. Does it mean that if the journalist "substantiates" that a private source *claims* the item has "news value," then it should be published? That is exactly what it says. Whether or not the item is true, or in fact *does* have news value, seems to matter not at all. Also, one might wonder about "news communications" from *public* sources, as well as "private sources"; would SDX'ers not want to check them out?

On and on goes the Code, setting up guidelines for the organization-persons. Truth is mentioned as the ultimate goal; then objectivity in reporting is set up as another goal, although it would seem this is tautological. The SDX'er is told that "there is no excuse for inaccuracies or lack of thoroughness," although he knows, if he manages to think at all for himself, that there are *plenty* of excuses for inaccuracies and that "lack of thoroughness" is so vague as to be meaningless. He knows that *no* report is thorough; it is all a matter of degree, and SDX, unfortunately, does not tell the journalist how much thoroughness is enough.

Then we are told by the Code that "news reports should be free of opinion or bias and represent all sides of an issue." This is a fascinating statement in its lack of realism or achievability. It is impossible to keep news reports free of opinion, and SDX journalists fill their stories every day with opinion of one kind or another—if not their own, then somebody else's. And, as to representing "all sides of an issue," any thoughtful reporter knows that there are any number of sides to issues (this is why they are issues), and that it is impossible to represent in any news report *all* sides of any issue. Journalists cannot even represent *all* *issues*, much less all sides of issues.

The Code goes into matters of "fair play," and states that journalists will respect "the dignity, rights and well-being of people encountered in the course of gathering and presenting the news," will "guard against invading a person's right to privacy," will not "pander to morbid curiosity about details of vice and crime," and will make prompt and complete correction of errors, and what is probably most interesting—that journalists will "be accountable to the public for their reports." Just what does this last "accountability" clause mean? How will journalists be accountable? This is the kind of language in journalistic codes which render them generally meaningless, or, at least, suspect.

Then, at the very end of the Code of Ethics, there is a "pledge." It reads as follows:

Journalists should actively censure and try to prevent violations

of these standards, and they should encourage their observance
by all newspeople. Adherence to this code of ethics is intended to
preserve the bond of mutual trust and respect between American
journalists and the American people.

Fair enough. But one thing is certain: the "bond of mutual trust"
might be preserved (if it is there) between journalists and
non-journalists in our society, but what about "mutual trust"
among journalists themselves? It is easy to imagine what would
happen if journalists took the "pledge" seriously and began
"actively" censuring their colleagues and trying to prevent
violations of this fuzzy and generalized Code of Ethics. Also the
thought occurs: If there is mutual trust and respect between
American journalists and the American people, how did it
develop without the Code of Ethics which SDX feels must
preserve it?

The real point of bringing up this Code here is to show that
really it is nothing more than high-sounding rhetoric; it may be
worthy of framing and hanging on the wall, but that is all. It
pretends to be "public" or "group" in its orientation—having a
kind of binding effect on SDX journalists—but it really is not a
legitimate code for this very reason. It can be nothing but
personal—as the individual interprets it—at its best; but when it
becomes "personal," it loses its reason for being. Why not simply
let the individual journalist frame his *own code* in his own words,
internally, and change it from time to time in his own time and in
his own way? The only valid ethics is that which is within each
person. The existential journalist knows this very well, and this
is why he cannot take seriously any normative ethical code,
however beautifully produced it may be.

                              *   *   *

Existentialism, by and large, is not very clear on the matter of
ethics; this is due, as was said earlier, to its personal nature.
Intrinsic in existentialism is the rebellion against firm rules and
collectivized standards. The *person* is enthroned, not the group.
As ethics comes into play in existentialism at all, it is an
individualistic ethics, a very personal thing. It leaves many
specific questions unanswered; in this sense, it cannot be forced
into the straightjacket of a "code." Hazel Barnes, in a book on
existentialist ethics, says, "The perfectly coherent, rigidly ob-

served code of ethics may well be maintained at the cost of foregoing all spontaneity."[21] She continues: "To be perfectly what one has chosen to be will inevitably exclude much that is precious in what he might otherwise have been."[22]

To some extent, the "pure" existentialist might say that the non-ethical choice is as good as the ethical choice—since both are authentic. But a good case can be made for choosing to be ethical. Hazel Barnes deals with this in these words:

> In insisting that one ought to choose to be ethical, we are on sure ground in affirming at least these things: First, the choice not to be ethical is almost wholly a rejection. Its bare minimum of positive value is the true recognition that one is in fact free not to subject himself to any demands whatsoever if he so chooses. . . . The purely nonethical life is as impossible to sustain practically as the perfectly ethical one. Insofar as it can be lived, it takes the form of rejecting all rational calculation, all responsibility for others and for one's own past and future—at least in the sense of feeling that one's acts should be governed by such considerations. It places all value on spontaneous self-realization and none on the temporal kind. Thus it is a choice of subjectivity and a rejection of objectivity, not an expansion of life but a reduction.[23]

So really, what we can say is that if a person chooses to be nonethical, he is choosing not-to-be or not-becoming; he is choosing Nothingness, and this is contrary to the ideals of the existentialist. The existentialist will choose to be ethical. And, as most existentialists say, rationality must be introduced as one of the criteria even though, as Barnes puts it, "it may at the same time insist that its goal is happiness or satisfaction or some other state which is closer to emotion than to reason."[24]

The importance of ethics to the existentialist is the degree to which we *act* ethically; a person may have all kinds of personal values—even down on paper (e.g., a Code of Ethics)—but one's actual life goes on as if the ethical did not exist. Existentialists—especially those taking their ethical cues from Kierkegaard—believe that the fundamental choice is not the choice between rival concepts of good and bad, but the "choice by which we

---

[21] Hazel E. Barnes, *An Existentialist Ethics* (New York: Random House Vintage Books, 1967), p. 21.

[22] *Ibid.*, p. 22.

[23] *Ibid.*, pp. 23-25 *passim*.

[24] *Ibid.*, p. 26.

summon good and bad into existence for ourselves."[25] Without such a choice, William Barrett says, an abstract system of ethics is just so "much paper currency with nothing to back it up."[26]

An individual can break with the ethical, "but he must have subordinated himself to the ethical universal; and the break, when he is called upon to make it, is made in fear and trembling and not in the callous arrogance of power," according to Barrett.[27] And the grounds for breaking with the ethical (in the sense of a kind of "social ethics"), to Kierkegaard, is the basic principle "that the individual is higher than the universal." As Barrett adds, "The universal rule of ethics, precisely because it is universal, cannot comprehend totally me, the individual, in my concreteness."[28] When something goes against a person's deepest self, then he is compelled to break (or transcend) the generally accepted ethics of his society; when one follows conscience he rises above ethics. "I am compelled to make an exception because I myself _am_ an exception; that is, a concrete being whose existence can never be completely subsumed under any universal or even system of universals," Barrett writes.[29] This "suspension of the ethical" is illustrated poignantly in Kierkegaard's story of Abraham and Isaac in _Fear and Trembling_.

Ethics must be personal if it is to contribute to the authenticity of the journalist. Following some group-designed code or traditional manner of action, either out of blind submission or thoughtless habit, is inauthentic and depersonalizing. Existentialism has often been criticized as a philosophical support for a kind of anarchical position in ethics; this, however, is unfair, for most conceptions of existentialism neither scorn rationality nor see the individual as detached from other individuals. In fact, in several existentialists (especially Sartre) there is a kind of Kantianism to be found: when the person chooses, they say, he is choosing not only for himself but for everybody. A similarity to Kant's Categorical Imperative can be noted here.

The basic point is this: no real blueprint exists for what the individual journalist can become, or what he should do. He must decide for himself. Each journalist's existence is his own. There is no universal pattern of journalism that can be imposed upon

---

[25] _Irrational Man_, p. 165.
[26] _Ibid._
[27] _Ibid._, p. 167.
[28] _Ibid._
[29] _Ibid._

him, to which he must conform. He must impose his own pattern on himself; but, more, he must constantly realize that this pattern will change—should change—and that his "demands upon himself" will be dynamic, not static.

A journalist becomes authentic, becomes truly himself, only to the extent that he freely chooses himself. His existence is authentic to the degree that he guides himself—or to the degree he has molded himself in his own individual image. The inauthentic journalist, on the contrary, is molded largely by external influences: circumstances, ethical codes, professional standards, habit, media authorities, or whatever. Of course, every journalist *must* be molded to some degree by outside forces; this is unavoidable. But the point here is that he *maximize* his own formation or molding and that he determine that these "depersonalizing" forces be held at arm's length. And this is a constant, full-time job, for the natural tendency is for him to conform, to slip into easy routine, and slowly lose personal authenticity.

But, many readers will ask, is not this orientation dangerous and unrealistic? Does it not lead to a complete relativism—even anarchy? In such a situation, how could morality have any real meaning for society? Are we going to end up with a kind of "chaos" in which every journalist "does his own thing"?

These questions suggest an unwarranted assumption about existentialism. No major existentialist philosopher has ever suggested that everything is permitted. Always there is some control. A kind of reasonableness, for instance, which will keep personal freedom in bounds, is quite common in existentialist literature. Or Christian "love," as in Kierkegaard's case, where a real concern for others keeps personal freedom under control. Or, as it is with Sartre, the control is exercised by his notion of responsibility. For as he sees it, the anguish of a choice arises from the fact that, in making the choice, a person is committing not only himself but, in a certain manner, all mankind. This, as has been suggested, is almost Kantian: one chooses then only those things which he would be willing to see universalized. This certainly keeps a rational person from going too far in "doing his own thing." Also—and this is important: the existential journalist *never* tries to escape the consequences for his authenticity, for his freely determined actions. There are always his superiors. He can always be fired. He must understand this; *he* alone must decide whether or not to take the risk.

Another Kantian concept creeps into existentialism. Camus

brings it up when he insists that every person must refuse to be treated as an object (*The Rebel*). To be treated as an object—or to treat others as objects—is an inauthentic situation, completely depersonalizing. Camus is implying that *all* is not permitted, and that the existential journalist, for example, must exercise controls on himself and must feel responsibility to others and a concern for others. The existentialist is not against controls; he simply rebels against these controls coming from *outside* agents.

Another check on the use of freedom is what Luka Brajnovic, a Yugoslav philosopher now teaching in Spain, calls "human dignity." He contends that this dignity places just limits on freedom for the simple reason that man does not live isolated in society; all members have this same human dignity.[30] And this human dignity he refers to, just what is it? We are told that the "moral man" has it. And who is this moral man? The man who does not succumb to his instincts or to his passions; who does not change his opinion without justification; is not a flatterer or renegade. Brajnovic calls all of these characteristics "monstrosities" which negate dignity, as well as the rights and the liberty of man.[31]

A person is also controlled by "conscience," however vague this concept may be. It may mean a person's awareness of the moral code accepted in his society, together with the feelings of discomfort or satisfaction that he may have as he either breaks or keeps the code. But it is also the term used for the kind of moral conviction that will sometimes lead a person to reject the accepted standards of his society in response to what he believes to be a more deeply rooted imperative. Existentialists tend to find more meaning in the second of these two senses; as has been mentioned earlier, Kierkegaard deals with "conscience" in this second sense in his *Fear and Trembling*. Nietzsche even goes further than Kierkegaard; he not only would suspend conventional moral obligations on occasion, but would transcend them completely. For him, the commonly accepted morality is like the "old broken tables" of the law; Nietzsche's concern is for the "Superman" who will go beyond man as he is.[32]

Heidegger seems to think of a "deeper conscience" that

[30] Luka Brajnovic, *Deontología Periodística* (Pamplona: Ediciones Universidad de Navarra, S.A., 1969), p. 151.

[31] *Ibid.*, p. 224.

[32] Macquarrie, *Existentialism*, p. 166.

delivers us from a kind of "public" conscience—from the moral dictates of "they." For Heidegger, true conscience summons the true self (*Dasein*) from its lostness in the "they." Only when the person stops listening to the voice of "they" can he truly hear the call of conscience, and become truly authentic. The source of this call? Heidegger suggests that it comes from the very depth of one's own being. It is the struggle of the authentic self to be born. And the "content" of the call? There is no content; it varies with the person, for each must seek to realize his own potentiality for being.[33]

In order to be more existential and more authentic, the journalist will promote in himself the basic Nietzschean theme of saying "yes to life" thereby becoming more noble and heroic— and thus more authentic.[34] The existential journalist would be something of a Nietzschean Superman—a person who has learned to transcend himself, to rise to his highest potential. He would be a "higher man"—a kind of law unto himself, a center of virtue, and a powerful, happy person of exuberant self-expression and self-confidence.[35] A key concept of Nietzsche, consistent with his existentialist orientation, is his passionate belief in the worth of the individual and his view of the hero as the person who does not submit to authority—or at least fights constantly against it.[36]

*   *   *

In conclusion, the point should be reemphasized that authenticity for the existential journalist comes from within; it rises up from the deep wells of the existent himself (*Dasein*) and it exhibits itself through actions which are taken deliberately and based on the absolute integrity of the journalist. Journalism educators and practicing journalists find themselves often living on inauthentic levels; on these levels they are evading choices and actions, they are speaking hypocritical words, they are

---

[33] *Ibid.*

[34] Karl Jaspers, *Nietzsche: An Introduction to the Understanding of His Philosophical Activity* (Chicago: Henry Regnery Co.—a Gateway Edition, 1969), p. 167 ff.

[35] See E. L. Allen, "The Superman" (Ch. 5) in *From Plato to Nietzsche* (Greenwich, Conn.: Fawcett Publications—a Premier Book, 1964), pp. 180-82.

[36] Bertrand Russell, *The Will to Doubt* (New York: Philosophical Library—the Wisdom Library, 1958), p. 101.

retreating from their own freedom, and they are refusing to make for themselves real existence.

In addition, they have refused to take responsibility for their own actions—or inactions, often shifting the blame to someone else. Too often, also, they have turned away from respect for themselves and have hidden in organizations, groups, societies and the like which seem to give them psychological relief from the anxieties and pain of authentic living. These teachers and journalists would be wise to heed the words of St. Augustine who wrote: *"Noli foras ire, in te redi, in interiore homine veritas habitat"*—"Do not desire to go out; return into yourself; truth lives within the inner man."[37]

---

[37] Edmund Husserl, *Cartesian Meditations*, trans. D. Cairns (The Hague: Nijhoff, 1960), p. 157.

Postscript:

Back to Newsroom and Academe

I tried your "existential journalism" on more than 20 editors and writers in my news room and one journalism faculty member at Chapel Hill. No one had ever heard the phrase before.

—C. A. McKNIGHT, Editor, *The Charlotte Observer* Charlotte, N.C.

Existential journalism is a phrase that has absolutely no meaning for me. I understand the generalized meanings of existential philosophy, but have not heard it applied to a particular form of journalism.

—JOE H. STROUD, Editor, *Detroit Free Press*

If "existential journalism" is taken to mean the type of journalism in which the journalist feels he/she can influence events and institutions by what he/she writes, then I can see some utility in the term. I would also, I think, probably consider that existential journalism would be the journalism of personal involvement, of intuitive writing about events, etc.

—AL HESTER, University of Georgia

I feel that existential journalism, without necessarily being conscious of itself as such, may become more prevalent if society continues to produce anxieties, dehumanization and cynicism (as opposed to skepticism) on as broad scale as currently.

—KARLEN MOORADIAN, University of Oklahoma

IN THIS SHORT CONCLUDING SECTION, I return to the responses to the questionnaire about existential journalism dealt with in the first chapter. Certainly there was a great deal of mystification evident in the responses from both newsroom and Academe. Practicing journalists (mainly editors) were perhaps a little vaguer than the professors in their conceptions of existential journalism, and definitely they were more bitter in many of their remarks. However, most journalism teachers evidenced similar frustration in trying to deal with the term which—admittedly—was a new one. It is interesting to note, nevertheless, that they considered existential journalism as a concept more important than did the practicing journalists.

Let's look briefly at some of the responses coming from the editors. And, at this point, I shall comment on some of them.

John Troutt, Jr., of the *Jonesboro* (Ark.) *Sun*, wrote that he did not have "the faintest idea what the term might mean." Then, with this sentence he struck the tone of most of his newsroom respondent colleagues—"I would also doubt that it is very important in the overall scheme of things." (It is interesting that he put it in this way, for as I have tried to show in the preceding pages, that the concept of "existential journalism" and how the individual journalist feels about it have *overriding importance* in the overall journalistic scheme of things.)

From the editor of *The News-Times* of Danbury, Conn., Robert J. Bailyn, came the advice to "define your terms." (This would have been difficult, of course, for me to do in that I was trying to find out what *he* thought "existential journalism" meant. If I had defined the term—which I have tried to do in this volume—there would have been no need for the questionnaire.) Bailyn informed me that nobody in his newsroom had any notion of what "existential journalism" meant. Then he proceeded to pose this question: "Is it that we here are locked in the private hell of our newsroom, condemned to face each other and our-selves for eternity, with no exit to Olympic journalistic thought?" (My answer to this question is "Yes, that is certainly the case." Whether he realizes it or not—or wants to face it or not—he and his staff *are* probably locked in "the private hell" of their newsroom, condemned to face each other and themselves—maybe not "for eternity," but for long enough.)

Ladd Hamilton, of the *Lewiston* (Idaho) *Morning Tribune*, got right to the point: "I never use the term and don't know what it means." And that was it. (I hope that he will learn what it means, and I am happy that, since he didn't know what it meant, he never used it.) Then Hamilton proceeded to decry the fact that he was "getting people out of journalism schools who can't spell,[1] who can't compose a lead and never heard of libel." He added: "and you ask me to share your concern about existential journalism." (Actually, however, it was his *definition* of the term, not my *concern*, that I asked him to share with me.) He put into words what obviously many of the journalists surveyed were thinking, when he wrote: "I doubt whether it [existential jour-nalism] has anything to do with the real world of writing and editing—or the teaching thereof." (Mr. Hamilton *doubts;* I, on the other hand, *know* that it most certainly *does* have something to do with "the real world of writing and editing—and, as I tried to show in the last chapter, also with "the teaching thereof.")

Mike Lavelle, of *The Chicago Tribune*, wrote that if I were to catch him when he is in his sixties he might be able to define what he has been doing in "heavy metaphysical terms," but for the present, he said, he is too busy doing whatever he does to bother with what he thinks he thinks he is doing. Then he proceeded to remark that "the trend that disturbs" him is the "prevalence of irrelevant questionnaires like this one." (I am sorry this "trend," as he calls it, disturbs him. If he were truly an existential journalist, this "trend"—even if it were that—would

---

[1] Several editors other than Mr. Hamilton complained about journalism students' writing and spelling. And in the process of complaining, some of them spelled atrociously in their responses. I was tempted to quote them verbatim (without doctoring their comments), but felt this would be unfair since presum-ably they were writing without any real interest in, or dedication to, the subject. Also, I'm sure many of them were writing rapidly and carelessly, not caring much for the questionnaire, and therefore were not producing up to their normal capacity.

pale to insignificance before far more disturbing problems which I'm sure must face him and his colleagues there at the *Tribune.*)

Jim Dance, associate editor of *The Miami Herald,* noted that despite his editorial department's "combined experience of more than 100 years in the newspaper business not a soul here has ever heard of nor can imagine what in the world 'existential journalism' is, are, or, as the case may be, were." Dance's remarks make a very important existential point, even though he may not have realized it, and that is that *years of experience* (or time in a job) does not mean anything when it comes to wisdom, knowledge, abilities, and creativity. What matters is what a person (or a whole staff) has been doing and thinking during that time.

"Alas, alas, I'm sorry to say the phrase 'existential journalism' has not penetrated to this isolated Eastern outpost," wrote Earl W. Foell, managing editor of *The Christian Science Monitor.* (Well, I hope that by now the term has so penetrated, and that it will make even more impact on the *CSM*, a newspaper which, knowing it or not, has been extremely existential over the years.) Foell added that at "the recent AP Managing Editors' conference in Williamsburg, where editors from across the country met for their annual discussion of journalistic issues, not a word was heard about 'existential journalism.'" (This, of course, does not surprise me in the least, having been to many conferences of journalists to observe their interests and antics. Probably the real existentialists among managing editors would not even be at such a conference. If they had been there, they would certainly have been concerned with the essence of "existential journalism," whether or not they used that specific term in their discourses.)

Now, let us turn to a few of the journalism professors and their comments about "existential journalism."

L. John Martin, of the University of Maryland, expressed ignorance of the term, but said that he guessed that the reference was to "the trend in subjective, descriptive journalism often referred to as new non-fiction." He proceeded to speculate that it would cover "any journalistic writing that is not primarily concerned with truth as an absolute but with truth as it is seen by the reporter." (I'm sure Dr. Martin realizes that *all* journalistic truth is "truth as it is seen by the reporter"; certainly, at least, the existential journalist realizes it.)

Martin continues, "Objectivity would be irrelevant in this existential type of journalism." (In one sense, of course, this is true, but as I have tried to explain in the preceding chapters, the existential journalist *is* seeking objectivity, but he simply recognizes that he must seek it subjectively. All reality, for him, is sifted through the reporter in his total subjectivity; there is no other kind of "reporting.") Then, Martin concludes with this sentence: "Objectivity is impersonal, while 'existential journalism' by this definition is very personal." (There is nothing to quarrel with here, except to say that the *objective world out there* (outside the reporter's consciousness) is, indeed, "objective"; but as soon as a reporter *reports* it, such objectivity evaporates—the report thus becoming "subjective." *All* reporters, actually, are very "personal," but the existentialist simply recognizes it and is not in the least ashamed of it.)

John DeMott, a professor at Temple University, is also concerned about the concept of "objectivity" when trying to discuss existential journalism. He wrote:

> Existential journalism is a contradiction in terms, really. Why? Because the essence of journalism is its objectivity. Now we all know, and concede readily, that no journalist can be 100 per cent objective. Or 100 per cent fair. Or truthful. Or accurate. Or anything else. However, an account of any "news" development is journalistic—rather than existential—it appears to me, to the degree that it corresponds to the relevant objective reality. If it's primarily an expression of the "reporter's" subjective reaction to the news event, or an opinion concerning it, then it's not journalism, in a professional sense.

DeMott goes on to say that he believes existential journalism (or something akin to it—with which he connects Norman Mailer, Jimmy Breslin, and the *Village Voice*) is becoming less and less prevalent; and for DeMott this is good, for he notes that "increased emphasis on objective reality, rather than the play world of periods like the late 1960s, is a boon." (Dr. DeMott seems to think of journalism and existentialism as mutually exclusive terms, and this, of course, is very far from the thesis of this volume; also he writes of the "play world" of periods like the late 1960s—I would maintain that that world was as *real* as, and no more of a "play world" than, any other period has been.)

One professor at a big Midwestern school of journalism responded that he was happy to see a "decline in 'ruleless' journalism, if it is declining and if that is a definition for existential journalism." But this professor would be sorry to see it fade completely, for, in his words, the "smug, established press got a useful jolt from the unconventional papers and could use some more." (I would certainly agree with the above conclusion, although the concept of "ruleless" journalism, as I have tried to show throughout these pages, does not do justice to the complexity of existential journalism.)

Patricia A. Larsen, of Central Missouri State University, wrote that she believed existential journalism is becoming more prevalent and that this trend is good. "But," she added, "it is good only if the journalist gives all sides of the issue, problem and story." Good reporters, she said, are "becoming involved in their stories, and investigative reporting demands involvement by the journalist, a total immersing into the story." (It is obvious that in this respondent's mind "existential journalism" is identified with investigative reporting. I hope that I have shown in this volume that it is much more than any technique or "type" of reporting—that it is an orientation or stance which a journalist takes in his total existence as a journalist.)

Donald A. Bird, of Central Michigan University, associated existential journalism with some forms of advocacy and New Journalism and believed that it was increasing. However, he felt that such a trend was unfortunate. David Rubin, of New York University, reported he had never heard of the term, nor had any of his media friends in New York. (I hope that they all have heard of it by now, or will very soon.) Wilbur L. Doctor, of the University of Rhode Island, said he had not heard of existential journalism and lamented: "Now I have to worry about what this deficiency in my education means." (It is strange that Professor Doctor, as many of the other respondents, seemed to think that I was asking if *they had heard of* (or were familiar with) *the term* "existential journalism"; what I asked was that they give a meaning that they attached to the term.)

Everette E. Dennis, of the University of Minnesota, was able to give his meaning to the term "existential journalism." He did it in these words:

> I think of it as a kind of mix of heart and head among intellectuals in journalism who tend to express themselves in thoughtful polemics.

(I would agree basically with this short characterization, but would not limit it to "intellectuals" in journalism.) Dennis went on to say that existential journalism, it seemed to him, would be at the opposite extreme of "precision journalism"[2] which in his words "moves journalism toward the rational-scientific." (It is strange how many people feel that an existentialist cannot be rational.)

Donald Ranly, of the University of Missouri, had no trouble giving his concept of existential journalism. In fact, he said that applying his knowledge of existentialism to "existential journalism" was not difficult: "The existential journalist does not give in to pressures, does not conform, is committed to being himself, to being free, and ultimately and always to the truth." According to Ranly, the percentage of existential journalists today is not high. "Most people," he wrote, "have their price" and abide by the motto: "Give us this day our daily compromise."

Ranly's definition of "existential journalism" is about as close to the essence of the definition which I have tried to develop in this volume as any of those provided by the respondents. And, since it is, it is perhaps a good one to end on; Ranly certainly shows that person with some basic knowledge of existentialism can, without too much difficulty, relate this knowledge to journalism and arrive at a meaningful concept of "existential journalism." Several other professors also did a thoughtful job of this in the brief space that they had.

The practicing journalists, on the other hand, with one or two exceptions, made no such effort. They were mainly concerned with evidencing their irritation at "academic questionnaires" in general, or with taking sarcastic jabs at the term "existential journalism" in particular. They felt generally that existential journalism—although they readily admitted they had no idea what it meant—was nothing really to be concerned about.

I feel certain that those persons who care nothing about the concept, who have a built-in bias against journalism education or academic concerns generally (and there are many such persons in journalism—and out) will probably *never* think existential journalism is important. Most of them will, in all probability, continue ignoring such "useless" concepts. And, most likely,

---

[2] The term "precision journalism" is taken from the the title of a popular book by Philip Meyer—*Precision Journalism: a Reporter's Introduction to Social Scientific Methods* (Bloomington: Indiana University Press, 1973).

even those who read this volume will still not be convinced of
the importance of existential journalism. Or, they will redefine
the term in their own ways—or brush off the term completely,
thinking it unnecessary or academically pretentious.

On the other hand, I know that the orientation described
here—an orientation which I am calling "existential journalism,"
will appeal to many persons. But, quite likely, they will be the
"already converted"—the existentialists who recognize the validity, the authenticity, the self-satisfaction, and daily challenge
that comes with such an orientation applied to journalistic
activities.

This volume has been mainly designed for those journalists
and journalism professors (and, of course, for the young people
who will be future journalists and journalism teachers) who are
concerned with philosophical concepts and problems in journalism. I hope that these pages will open new and interesting
vistas of thought for existentialists and non-existentialists alike,
and that dialogue in an area which I think is the most important
in journalism today will be expanded.

Existential or non-existential journalism?

Each journalist much choose.

Bibliography

Allen, E. L. *From Plato to Nietzsche*. Greenwich, Conn.: Fawcett Publications—a Premier Book, 1964.

Anderson, Jack. *The Anderson Papers*. New York: Random House—Ballentine Books, 1974.

Aranguren, J. L. *Human Communication*. Trans. by Frances Partridge. New York: McGraw-Hill, 1967.

Bagdikian, Ben. *The Effete Conspiracy and Other Crimes by the Press*. New York: Harper & Row—Colophon Books, 1974.

Barnes, Hazel. *An Existentialist Ethics*. New York: Random House—Vintage Books, 1971.

Barrett, William. *Irrational Man: A Study in Existential Philosophy*. New York: Doubleday Anchor Books, 1962.

_____ . *What is Existentialism?* New York: Grove Press, 1964.

Beauvoir, Simone de. *The Ethics of Ambiguity*. Trans. by Bernard Frechtman. Secaucus, N.J.: The Citadel Press, 1972.

Bell, A. Donald, and J. C. Merrill. *Dimensions of Christian Writing*. Grand Rapids, Mich.: Zondervan Publishing House, 1970.

Berger, Peter L. *Invitation to Sociology: A Humanistic* Perspective. Garden City, N.Y.: Doubdleday Anchor Books, 1963.

Bode, Carl (ed.). *The Portable Thoreau*. New York: The Viking Press, 1947.

Brajnovic, Luka. *Deontología Periodística*. Pamplona: Ediciones Universidad de Navarra, S.A., 1969.

Brée, Germaine. *Camus and Sartre: Crisis and Commitment*. New York: Dell Publishing Co.—a Delta Book, 1972.

Buber, Martin. *Between Man and Man*. Trans. by R. G. Smith. New York: The Macmillan Co., 1972.

Burnier, Michel-Antoine. *Choice of Action: The French Existentialists on the Political Front Line*. Trans. by B. Murchland. New York: Vintage Books, 1969.

Bury, J. B. *The Idea of Progress*. New York: The Macmillan Co., 1932.

Camus, Albert. *The Myth of Sisyphus & Other Essays.* Trans. by Justin O'Brien. New York: Vintage Books, 1955.

_____. *The Rebel.* New York: Alfred Knopf, Inc., and Random House—Vintage Books, 1954.

_____. *Resistance, Rebellion, and Death.* Trans. by Justin O'Brien. New York: Random House—Vintage Books, 1961.

_____. *The Stranger.* New York: Vintage Books, 1946.

Collins, James. *The Mind of Kierkegaard.* Chicago: Henry Regnery Co.—a Gateway Edition, 1967.

Danto, Arthur C. *Jean-Paul Sartre.* New York: The Viking Press, 1975.

Dennis, Everette E. and William L. Rivers. *Other Voices: The New Journalism in America.* San Francisco: The Canfield Press, 1974.

Ellul, Jacques. *Propaganda.* New York: Vintage Books, 1973.

Epstein, Edward J. *Between Fact and Fiction: The Problem of Journalism.* New York: Random House—Vintage Books, 1975.

Frankel, Charles. *The Case for Modern Man.* Boston: Beacon Press, 1971.

Frings, Manfred S. (ed.). *Heidegger and the Quest for Truth.* Chicago: Quadrangle Books, 1968.

Fromm, Erich. *Escape from Freedom.* New York: Avon Books, 1965.

_____. *Man for Himself.* Greenwich, Conn.: A Fawcett Premier Book, 1966.

_____. *The Revolution of Hope.* New York: Harper & Row, 1968.

Gardner, John W. *Excellence.* New York: Harper & Row—Perennial Library, 1971.

Grene, Marjorie. *Introduction to Existentialism.* Chicago: University of Chicago Press, 1970.

Harris, Sydney J. *The Authentic Person: Dealing with Dilemma.* Niles, Ill.: Argus Communications, 1972.

Heinemann, F. H. *Existentialism and the Modern Predicament.* New York: Harper Torchbooks, 1958.

Hill, Brian V. *Education and the Endangered Individual.* New York: Dell Publishing Co., 1973.

Hoffer, Eric. *The True Believer.* New York: Mentor Books, 1962.

Horvath, Nicholas A. *Philosophy.* Woodbury, N.Y.: Barron's Educational Series, Inc., 1974.

Huizinga, Johan. *Homo Ludens.* Boston: Beacon Press, 1955.

Husserl, Edmund. *Cartesian Meditations.* The Hague: Nijhoff, 1960.

Huxley, Aldous. *Brave New World Revisited.* New York: Harper & Row—Perennial Library, 1965.

Jaspers, Karl. *Man in the Modern Age.* Garden City, N.Y.: Doubleday Anchor Books, 1957.

_____. *Neitzsche: An Introduction to the Understanding of His Philosophical Activity.* Chicago: Henry Regnery Co.—a Gateway Edition, 1969.

Johnson, Michael L. *The New Journalism.* Lawrence: University of Kansas Press, 1971.

Jung, Carl G. *The Undiscovered Self.* New York: Mentor Books, 1958.

Jung, Hwa Yol (ed.). *Existential Phenomenology and Political Theory: A Reader.* Chicago: Henry Regnery Co., 1972.

Kaplan, Abraham. *The New World of Philosophy.* New York: Vintage Books, 1961.

Kaufmann, Walter (ed.). *Existentialism from Dostoevsky to Sartre.* New York: New American Library—Medidian Books, 1975.

Kierkegaard, Søren. *Fear and Trembling* and *The Sickness unto Death.* Trans. by Walter Lowrie. Princeton: Princeton University Press, 1968.

———. *The Present Age.* New York: Harper Torchbooks, 1962.

Klein, J. F. *The Physical Significance of Entropy.* New York: D. Van Nostrand Co., 1919.

Koestenbaum, Peter. *Philosophy: A General Introduction.* New York: American Book Co., 1968.

Kuhns, William. *The Post-Industrial Prophets: Interpretations of Technology.* New York: Harper Colophon Books, 1971.

Macquarrie, John. *Existentialism.* Baltimore: Penguin Books, 1973.

Mannheim, Karl. *Ideology and Utopia.* New York: Harcourt Brace and Co., 1936.

Mansur, Anthony. *Sartre: a Philosophic Study.* New York: Oxford University Press, 1967.

Marcel, Gabriel. *Man Against Mass Society.* Chicago: Henry Regnery Co.—a Gateway Edition, 1969.

———. *The Philosophy of Existentialism.* Trans. by Manya Harari. New York: The Citadel Press, 1968.

Marcuse, Herbert. *One-Dimensional Man.* Boston: Beacon Press, 1966.

McLuhan, Marshall. *Understanding Media: The Extensions of Man.* New York: McGraw-Hill Paperbacks, 1965.

McQuail, Denis (ed.). *Sociology of Mass Communications.* Baltimore: Penguin Books, 1972.

Mencken, H. L. *A Gang of Pecksniffs.* Edited by Theo Lippman, Jr. New Rochelle, N.Y.: Arlington House, 1975.

Merleau-Ponty, Maurice. *Adventures of the Dialectic.* Trans. by Joseph Bien. Evanston: Northwestern University Press, 1973.

———. *Phenomenology of Perception.* Trans. by Colin Smith. London: Routledge & Kegan Paul, 1962.

Merrill, John C. *The Imperative of Freedom: A Philosophy of Journalistic Autonomy.* New York: Hastings House, 1974.

Merrill, John C., and Ralph L. Lowenstein. *Media, Messages, and Men.* New York: David McKay, 1971.

Meyer, Philip. *Precision Journalism: A Reporter's Introduction to Social Scientific Methods.* Bloomington: Indiana University Press, 1973.

Middleton, Neil (ed.). *The I. F. Stone's Weekly Reader.* New York: Vintage Books, 1974.

Existential Journalism

Mills, C. Wright. *Power, Politics and People.* New York: Ballantine Books, 1962.

Morgan, George W. *The Human Predicament.* New York: Dell Publishing Co.—a Delta Books, 1970.

Mumford, Lewis. *Transformations of Man.* New York: Harper Torchbooks, 1972.

Needham, Joseph. *Time: The Refreshing River.* New York: Macmillan, 1943.

Nietzsche, Friedrich. *The Birth of Tragedy* and *The Case of Wagner.* Trans. by Walter Kaufmann. New York: Vintage Books, 1967.

_____. *On the Genealogy of Morals* and *Ecce Homo.* Trans. by Walter Kaufmann. New York: Vintage Books, 1967.

_____. *Twilight of the Idols* and *The Anti-Christ.* Trans. by R. J. Hollingdale. Baltimore: Penguin Books, 1974.

Novack, George (ed.). *Existentialism versus Marxism.* New York: Dell Publishing Co.—Delta Books, 1966.

Novak, Michael. *Belief and Unbelief: A Philosophy of Self-Knowledge.* New York: Mentor-Omega Books, 1965.

_____. *The Experience of Nothingness.* New York: Harper Colophon Books, 1971.

Olson, Robert G. *An Introduction to Existentialism.* New York: Dover Publications, Inc., 1962.

Ortega y Gasset, José. *Man and People.* New York: W. W. Norton & Co., 1963.

_____. *Mission of the University.* New York: W. W. Norton & Co.—The Norton Library, 1944.

Patka, Frederick (ed.). *Existentialist Thinkers and Thought.* New York: The Citadel Press, 1966.

Poole, Roger, *Towards Deep Subjectivity.* New York: Harper Trochbooks, 1972.

Riesman, David. *The Lonely Crowd.* New Haven: Yale University Press, 1961.

Roubiczek, Paul. *Existentialism: For and Against.* Cambridge: Cambridge University Press, 1966.

Russell, Bertrand. *Authority and the Individual.* Boston: Beacon Press, 1960.

_____. *The Will to Doubt.* New York: Philosophical Library—the Wisdom Library, 1958.

Sartre, Jean-Paul. *Being and Nothingness.* New York: Philosophical Library, 1956.

_____. *Existentialism and Human Emotions.* New York: Philosophical Library, 1957.

_____. *Situations.* Trans. by Nenita Eisler. Greenwich, Conn.: A Fawcett Premier Book, 1965.

Schiller, Herbert I. *Mass Communications and American Empire.* Boston: Beacon Press, 1971.

Seidenberg, Roderick. *Posthistoric Man: An Inquiry.* New York: Viking Press, 1974.

Solomon, Robert C. (ed.). *Phenomenology and Existentialism.* New York: Harper & Row, 1972.

Solzhenitsyn, Alexander. *From Under the Rubble.* New York: Bantam Books, 1975.

Sorokin, Pitirim A. *Modern Historical and Social Philosophies.* New York: Dover Publications, Inc., 1963.

Spengler, Oswald. *The Decline of the West.* New York: Alfred A. Knopf, Inc., 1926.

_____. *Selected Essays.* Trans. by Donald O. White. Chicago: Henry Regnery Co.—a Gateway Edition, 1967.

Streller, Justus. *To Freedom Condemned: A Guide to the Philosophy of Jean-Paul Sartre.* New York: Philosophical Library—the Wisdom Library, 1960.

Tebbel, John. *The Media in America.* New York: New American Library—Mentor Books, 1976.

Trilling, Lionel. *Sincerity and Authenticity.* Cambridge: Harvard University Paperback, 1972.

Tuccille, Jerome. *Radical Libertarianism.* New York: Perennial Library, 1971.

Van Over, Raymond (ed.). *The Psychology of Freedom.* Greenwich, Conn.: Fawcett Premier Books, 1974.

Volkman, A. D. (ed.). *Thoreau on Man and Nature.* Mt. Vernon, N.Y.: The Peter Pauper Press, 1960.

Wahl, Jean. *A Short History of Existentialism.* New York: Philosophical Library, 1949.

White, Morton. *Social Thought in America: The Revolt Against Formalism.* Boston: Beacon Press, 1957.

Wiener, Norbert. *The Human Use of Human Beings: Cybernetics and Society.* New York: Avon Books—Discus Edition, 1967.

Wolfe, Tom. *The New Journalism.* New York: Harper & Row, 1973.

Wylie, Philip. *The Magic Animal.* New York: Simon & Schuster—Pocket Books, 1969.

Yablonsky, Lewis. *Robopaths: People as Machines.* Baltimore: Penguin Books, 1972.

Index

Accuracy in Media (AIM), 9
Action, existential journalistic, 115-17
Adams, Henry, 85
Addison, Joseph, 60
Alienation, 68, 69-71
All the President's Men (film), 9
Allen, E. L., 137*n*.
American Society of Newspaper Editors, 64
Anderson, Jack, 77 and *n*.
Anderson Papers, The 77*n*.
Angst (anxiety), 66, 69, 72, 73, 74, 83
"Anguish," and existentialism, 55, 56, 70
Anomie, 68
Anouilh, Jean, 12, 13
Anxiety (*Angst*), 66, 69, 72, 73, 74, 83
Atlanta Journal, 26
Atlanta Journal-Constitution Magazine, 27
Augustine, St., 138
Authenticity, 118-19; as elusive goal, 119-21; and ethics, 129-38; in journalism education, 121-29
Authoritarianism, 66, 83

"Bad faith," 56, 65, 89, 95
Bagdikian, Ben, 77 and *n*.
Bailyn, Robert J., 140-41; quoted, 26, 140, 141
Barnes, Hazel E., 43, 132, 133*n*.; quoted, 133

Barrett, William, 44 and *n*., 52, 94*n*., 99, 127*n*., 134
Being and Nothingness (Sartre), 22, 95*n*., 105*n*.
Belief and Unbelief: A Philosophy of Self-Knowledge (Novak), 113*n*.
Bell, A. Donald, 40*n*.
Bell, Thomas, 105
Berdyaev, Nikolai, 57, 89, 90, 91, 94, 119; quoted, 94
Berger, Peter, 126 and *n*.
Berkeley Barb, 32
Berry, B. R., 63*n*.; quoted, 64
Between Fact and Fiction: The Problem of Journalism (Epstein), 77*n*.
Bird, Donald A., 144
Birth of Tragedy from the Spirit of Music, The (Nietzsche), 38
Bode, Carl, 82*n*., 100*n*.
Boltzmann, Ludwig, 87
Brajnovic, Luka, 136 and *n*.
Brave New World Revisited (Huxley), 20*n*., 68
Brée, Germaine, 61*n*., 120, 121
Breslin, Jimmy, 32, 143
Buber, Martin, 109, 119
Bulletin, The (ASNE), 19*n*., 62*n*., 63*n*.
Bury, J. B., 84*n*.

Camus, Albert, 12, 26, 32, 53, 58 and *n*., 60, 61 and *n*., 62, 70, 80, 119, 120, 121, 135, 136; quoted, 97